The Rapture Revisited

Finally, a Lawyer Takes a Look at End-Time Events

Blessings
Bob Walter
Jan 21, 2018

φ

S-E-L-F PUBLISHING

Simple-Effective-Literary-Focusing on Publishing
10120 W. Flamingo Rd.
Suite 4 #228
Las Vegas, NV 89147

Visit us at www.yourpublisher.org

ISBN 978-0-9969201-7-9

Printed In The United States Of America
10 9 8 7 6 5 4 3 2

The Rapture Revisited

Finally, a Lawyer Takes a Look at End-Time Events"

Rob Walter

℘

S-E-L-F PUBLISHING

Simple- Effective-Literary-Focusing on Publishing

Dedication

I dedicate this book to all my grandchildren who will need to be strong in the Lord for the dark days ahead, days darker than my generation has faced but brighter when you come of age to know that God has called you for just such a time as this.

You can do it and you will do it because you serve a mighty God. If God be for you and He is, then who can be against you?

Acknowledgments

Thank you to my wife Lisa who provided the most in-depth review and edit suggestions I could possibly expect. She knows well the passion I have developed for this topic and her contribution has facilitated the honing and fine-tuning of that passion.

I would also like to thank my son Ryan who wrote his first book several years ago and in so doing, unintentionally shamed me into getting off my duff and do likewise.

Introduction

Let's start with a confession. This is a book that I had neither intended, nor desired to write. But events have a way of changing our plans or should I say that God has a way of ordering events that redirects our plans. In many respects, this book is the product of a reluctant submission to a calling that has dogged me for years. This calling has been an annoyance to my spirit and more recently a vexation that has cried out for relief. This book is that relief for me and I trust an inspiration and revelation to you.

By the time I graduated from high school I still had not been in a single honest-to-goodness fistfight. Not because I was afraid but largely because I simply had not encountered a situation of sufficient gravity (or a contested girl that attracted me enough) that warranted bloodying my knuckles. When a situation would arise, I would deflect and remove myself and sometimes the antagonist would continue to pursue me. When the day came to take a stand against an individual who was single-handedly destroying my high school experience, I finally responded instead of avoiding the challenge. He was so stunned that he backed off, we became mild friends and I dare say that if I had been subsequently accosted by anyone, he may well have come to my defense.

We have a radio station here in California that my wife has dubbed the "all-pre-tribulation-rapture" station. Many would say that maybe God has been trying to teach me something and that I should listen to these individuals and subscribe to their teaching. I did that for 15 years and since those years of subscribing to a pre-tribulation rapture position, I have avoided direct confrontation over the issue. But alas, I have ended up in a box canyon and engagement is unavoidable. I can't remove myself any longer. Of course, these individuals have not personally targeted me and the fistfight analogy obviously overstates the tension. Furthermore, and without question, many of those engaged in their intense advocacy of what I consider "escapism theology" are well-intentioned, God-loving, true Christians. But "iron sharpens iron" and this book is that long-postponed engagement.

Without years of increasing vexation over this issue, I doubt that I would have come to the realization of the truly monumental importance of the truths that needed to be shared in this book. A purpose of less magnitude would not have caused the cyclical anxiety that now drives me to finally address this topic. But accepted or rejected, what has needed to be said, I have finally said. To that end, I truly hope that at least some of you reading this book, who have subscribed to a pre-tribulation rapture theory will, one day, should I be accosted for embracing a post-tribulation rapture position, come to my defense.

Suggestions

I'm not sure that a book has ever had a section on "Suggestions" but this is not a typical book. At times, the material is complex and to the best of my ability, I have simplified the concepts as much as I can. None of this suggests that most readers are incapable of digesting meaty topics. On the contrary, the challenge for me has been how to unpack the confusing and sometimes complex reasoning behind the pre-tribulation rapture arguments without getting entangled in the same web. When something is convoluted it can get messy "unconvoluting" it. So to that end, may I suggest the following:

1. Have your Bible handy and when particular Scripture verses covered in some detail arise, read the passages as well from your own Bible. It will help with the context.

2. If a chapter or certain concepts are particularly difficult to digest, then stop with that chapter for the day but read it twice. The toughest chapters are 6, 7, and 8. They aren't long though and you will grasp significantly more reading them a second time. In law school there were times

I just couldn't get my arms around a difficult concept or case and simply had to reread it until the light broke through. I may be slower than many of you but persistence will yield its fruit. I promise.

3. The chapters really bear no chronology, except for the final chapter. If you get bogged down, then move on and come back later.

4. Mark up the book profusely. If you disagree with something, then note it in the margin and conversely make note of "ah hah" excerpts. You will use this book as a reference for the rest of your life.

If you desire to contact me, please send your comments to info@redskyradio.net.

Thank you for investing the time to understand a topic that is far more important than I had originally thought it to be. And whatever you do, finish the book.

Content

Dedication
Acknowledgement
Introduction
Suggestions

CHAPTER 1

THE NEED FOR EVIDENCE

Evidence is the heart of every lawyer's case. It is said that when the facts are not in your favor, argue the law, and when the law is not in your favor, argue the facts. But in either situation, the strength of any position ultimately depends upon the quality of the evidence. As a Christian, I need no evidence from God regarding the truth of His Word other than the simple fact that He said it. However, when man draws conclusions from God's Word and thereby establishes certain precepts as foundational, then I need proof that those conclusions are supported by evidence. How that evidence is assembled, its order, consistency, logic and degree of confirmation elsewhere in the Word, are all factors in assessing the quality (and hence, persuasiveness) of such evidence.

A basic principle of evidence is that the more important the issue, the greater the burden of proof required in order to justify the remedy being sought. For example, a civil trial involving a lawsuit against a city for damage done to your house because a dead tree belonging to the city fell on it requires a lesser burden of proof than convicting someone of murder. One involves monetary loss. The other involves possible loss of life (capital punishment) or loss of liberty (imprisonment). As such, it demands a higher probability of guilt that the accused is in fact responsible than the probability that the city knew or should have known that their tree was dead. This distinction is biblical. No one (biblically) can be executed for certain crimes except upon the testimony of two (and preferably three) witnesses. That number of witnesses is not required for lesser punishments in Scripture.

As we are admonished to not dispute doubtful things, some matters are not worthy of discussion and when discussed likely lead to unnecessary division in the body. Other matters are of monumental importance, such as the veracity of Jesus' resurrection. But in between are a host of matters of varying degrees of importance. One such "tweener" is the issue of the timing of the rapture. As noted in the Introduction, this is not an issue I would invest time in other than the fact that over the years, the extreme emphasis placed upon this topic by some of those who support the notion of a pre-tribulation rapture has drawn me into the fray. The repetitive, if not incessant teaching of the doctrine on the West Coast by various denominations has caught my attention. Possibly, this matter is more important than I had previously considered.

If a pre-tribulation doctrine is that important and it's true, then I need to give it more attention. If it's not true and the consequences of teaching error can cause material damage to the Body of Christ, then others need to know that as well. Assuming the apparent importance of the doctrine, the biblical support for a doctrine of that importance demands a higher level of evidence. In other words, those who advocate so strongly for acceptance of the pre-tribulation rapture doctrine have, by their own level of advocacy, heightened their own burden of proof. If the advocates were less demanding of me, I may demand less evidence from them.

But before we proceed further, several observations are in order. When a person accepts the Lord, everything is new as it says in II Corinthians 5:17, KJV:

> "Therefore if any man be in Christ, he is a new creature: old things are passed away; behold, all things are become new."

When a person is cleansed from all sin, the newness of everything (and newness of our perspective of everything) is almost overwhelming. Second, while everything is new, some things stay the same. It's not a contradiction. I'm speaking about certain character or personality traits that may be hardwired.

If a person was an extrovert before accepting the Lord, he or she is likely still an extrovert. It's just that now the person's positive and gregarious nature is redirected. A pensive person is still pensive but now thinks deeply about different things. I'm not suggesting that unhealthy habits or destructive behavioral attitudes remain unchecked or unchanged but rather that those God-given attributes that make each of us unique simply have a new and different application on the other side of salvation.

So as one who placed a premium on logic, correctness, order and literalness before I accepted the Lord as Savior, those attributes were right there, ready to go to work in me after salvation. I don't demand evidence for biblical propositions because I went to law school. I went to law school because I have always demanded evidence for substantive propositions of all kinds when it's man making the propositions. Trust me, I'm hard on myself. Logic, order and literalness (i.e., words mean things) were hardwired. So the practice of law has only given form to the traits God has given me. I say this to make the point that the following analysis of the timing of the rapture is not an attempt to puncture one theory or the other. I'm simply subjecting this apparently very important topic to the scrutiny demanded of anything so intensely advocated.

I am not a theologian. I'm an attorney and we'll be looking at the evidentiary basis for a pre-tribulation rapture. It is neither my intention nor my gifting to nuance each passage for possible explanations from a theological perspective. The Bible is a covenant. A covenant is a contract. God is the best contract drafter and a good drafter of contracts does not purposefully introduce ambiguities, contradictions or confusion. The intent of a well-drafted contract flows naturally from the text and a good contract ultimately is one that can be interpreted on its face. My primary purpose is not to prove a post-tribulation rapture (though that's what I believe Scripture clearly reveals) but rather to establish that a pre-tribulation rapture is *not* provable. Part of proving its incorrectness necessarily involves showing proof of a post-tribulation rapture because the lack of support for a pre-tribulation rapture cannot be discussed and debunked in a vacuum and the post-tribulation explanation nicely fills that vacuum.

CHAPTER 2

LET'S ASSUME THERE IS A PRE-TRIBULATION RAPTURE

When I accepted Jesus Christ as my Lord and Savior, numerous people suggested that I get a Bible and begin reading in the Gospels, and in particular, the Book of John. I was perplexed. Why would I start reading three quarters of the way through the Bible? Among other things, the Bible is a manual for living and it made no more sense, for me to start reading the Bible somewhere in the New Testament than it would for me, today, to start reading the owner's manual for my Kubota tractor on page 28. As an attorney, I can't conceive of beginning the review of a client's contract with paragraph 14. If God is a God of order (which He is) and since a testament is a covenant or contract, it only seemed logical when I became a Christian to begin, alas, at the beginning. If God started in Genesis, then I was going to start in Genesis, Elizabethan English and all.

It should be noted at the outset that I cannot underscore enough the importance of studying the entirety of the Old Testament, beginning with the Book of Genesis. I received a call from a nice woman who knew about our prison ministry at church and wanted to give us a large supply of New Testament paperbacks. I kindly passed on the offer. The last thing I wanted to convey to the prisoners was that somehow the Old Testament was, well, old and need not be read and applied or maybe worse yet, imply the condescending notion that prisoners somehow lacked the intelligence or commitment to read and understand the Old Testament. So, it's with particular gratification when I receive letters from prisoners with generous quotes from the Old Testament, revealing an understanding of the Scriptures that apply to events in the world today. The substance and insight reflected in these letters often surpasses the understanding of the Word by those "on the outside."

It's called the Old Testament because it was written before the New Testament, not because it's been replaced. Certain rituals and ordinances have been "nailed to the cross" because of the blood of Jesus and are no longer applicable but so much still is relevant. Even the dietary laws are not without merit. So much of the Old Testament has direct and immediate application for us that we ignore it at our peril. The unbiblical positions embraced by many Christians today on a host of issues are the direct result of an embarrassing and abysmal ignorance of the instruction and direction contained in the Old Testament. All that to say this: read the entire Bible and read it chronologically. There's a purpose to its order and you will see how end-time events more clearly come into place in so doing.

So, I started in Genesis and off I went. Lo and behold, I immediately ran into a God of order. Day one of creation preceded day two and guess what? Day two preceded day three. Taking Scripture literally unless there was an obvious reason to do otherwise was natural to me, so the thought of things such as evolution requiring a metaphorical description could not have been farther from my mind. When my Heavenly Father speaks, I receive it literally, whether I understand it or not. I trust that if I believe, then, at an appointed time, the understanding will follow.

As a new Christian, there was a tendency to receive as gospel anything anyone said who had been a Christian eight minutes longer than I. At one point, I even spent my entire savings on a set of teaching tapes that I devoured while filling three notebooks. Thus, it was inevitable, as with most new Christians, the time would come when I would want to understand how everything played out in the end. What's ahead? And with that, I consumed anything I could get my hands on regarding the rapture, Jesus' return to earth and the Great Tribulation.

A quick word is in order at this point regarding terms. People frequently use the word "Tribulation" and the term "Great Tribulation" interchangeably. Jesus uses the term "great tribulation" in Matthew 24:21 as the time period of three and one-half years following the abomination of desolation spoken of in verse 15. The second half of Daniel's last week (one "week" constituting the seven years preceding Jesus' return) is clearly more intense than the first three and one-half years. PTR apologists refer to the entire seven-year period as the time of tribulation and I will also.

Just how bad the first three and one-half years are we don't know. What we do know is that after the anti-Christ's unveiling halfway through those seven years, things intensify. Therefore the references to the two terms will be as follows: when "tribulation" is referred to it will be in the context of persecution anywhere in the world either before or after the beginning of the last seven years, as the context dictates. "Great Tribulation" will refer to the heightened level of persecution during the final three and one-half years prior to Jesus' return. Great Tribulation will, in this context, include persecution of both Jew and Christian alike during that time period.

So, with this newly acquired inquisitiveness, I assumed everything I was taught was correct; however, that is until one day when I could no longer make sense of Matthew 24 (which will be discussed in detail later). At least I couldn't make sense of it anymore in the context of a pre-tribulation rapture, that being the belief that seven years prior to Jesus return, Christians will be instantly removed from earth and thereby escape the Great Tribulation and all that Satan would visit upon them during this period. The Bible clearly states Satan will be openly hostile toward Christians and Jews. So I scheduled meetings with my pastor, who would suggest this book or that teaching, all of which caused me greater consternation because of one overriding concern. The pre-tribulation rapture position just didn't flow logically from the text and I had to jump around (as in abandon chronology) to try and fit Scripture into the pre-tribulation schematic. There were just too many twists and turns that were required to come up with a pre-tribulation rapture conclusion. It just didn't make sense without having to employ scriptural gymnastics. If you gave a special meaning to this passage and then tweaked that passage and then gave another verse a somewhat arbitrary meaning, then it would finally provide the intended conclusion of getting us out of here early. The more I studied, the more it seemed that the pre-tribulation rapture perspective started with the assumption of its truth but then required rearranging the chronology of scriptures and ignoring logical interpretations to fit a pre-determined conclusion.

The problem was that the pre-tribulation rapture suit just did not fit. Only by shortening a leg here, lengthening a sleeve there and other unnatural tailoring could I make it fit, but then it only fit if I was comfortable walking around in a contorted posture. All the subtle meanings and special interpretations could no longer convince me, or a biblical jury in my opinion, that the evidence even remotely came close to compelling a verdict in favor of a pre-tribulation rapture.

If this were a contract case, a jury could never get to the meaning ascribed to various passages by pre-tribulation rapture apologists. Conversely, a jury could readily accept a post-tribulational interpretation though, since that is the natural order and flow of the text.

An anecdotal comment needs to be inserted here. Over the last 25 years or so, I have not met one single person who believed in a pre-tribulation rapture who got there solely by reading Scripture. They may exist but I have yet to meet that person. Everyone who embraces a pre-tribulation rapture position, with whom I have talked, embraces it because of someone else's teaching. Is it because people don't naturally lift pre-tribulation perspectives from the text without significant help or instruction first coming from others? Is that also why it requires constant reinforcement?

If you are a "pre-trib" rapture person, ask yourself, honestly, by what means did you come to believe this position? Entirely independent of any teaching on what to think, were you just reading through Scripture one day and concluded, "Oh my gosh, we're going to be raptured before things get really bad!" No, you were taught that perspective. Conversely, I don't know that I have ever met a post-tribulation rapture person who embraces that position *primarily* because of the teaching of others. They are where they are, as I suspect I am, because in the reading of Scripture many times, the natural and orderly flow of the text of Scripture simply leads the reader to a post-tribulation view. It was the natural flow that caused my conversion after many years of trying to make that suit fit. The way I saw it was that God wouldn't draft a confusing contract.

I had embraced the pre-tribulation rapture (hereinafter "PTR") position for 15 years but it had become more and more unsettling in my spirit. It was all I had been exposed to and never had I heard of a post-tribulation rapture perspective. Accelerating my migration out of the PTR camp however, was a lecture I attended in my second year of law school in Tulsa, Oklahoma. It was a voluntary, non-law lecture that I really didn't want to go to at which Richard Wurmbrand was speaking, a man I had never heard of nor did I really care to hear. As a Romanian Messianic Jew, Mr. Wurmbrand (the founder of Voice of the Martyrs ministry) began to describe his ordeal after WWII and during the communist occupation and the trauma suffered while in prison in Romania. He suffered because of the horrific and despicable crime of preaching Yeshua in public. With that he had me.

While I don't remember the exact details of his lecture, the essence of his prison life was one of beating, starvation and torture followed by more beating, starvation and torture. He talked about being hungry and cold in a dark damp cell and then trying to get to sleep before the guards would open up a little door in the wall and let in purposefully starved rats. He was sleep deprived for hours and he would fend off the rats lying in the fetal position as they nibbled on his ear lobes, toes and any area of his body with soft tissue. Then I pondered the unspeakable. I imagined visiting him in his prison cell and telling him to be of good cheer because he would not have to endure the Great Tribulation since he would be raptured before he would have to truly suffer. Even in my imagination Mr. Wurmbrand was too much of a gentlemen to take a swing at me though he would have been entitled to do so. That day moved me ever so close to the tipping point.

There are so many people that I truly love who have embraced the PTR position that I say with all humility, the issue is not one that separates those who will go to heaven from those who won't. But sadly, there are some PTR advocates who regard those who don't subscribe to the PTR teaching as virtual heretics. I have wondered why that is so. There are a number of churches that include the PTR as part of their Statement of Beliefs. A Statement of Beliefs invariably focuses upon that which is considered foundational such as the virgin birth of Jesus, Christ's atoning work on the cross, His resurrection and the infilling of the Holy Spirit. If one disagreed with any of the foregoing core beliefs, they would be deemed a heretic and I would concur. But when you include the PTR as part of the core beliefs, it then becomes a heretical position to not so subscribe. Of course, this is a tragic mistake in those churches as nothing concerning the PTR even remotely involves the issue of one's salvation or belief in the indisputable and essential core beliefs of Christianity.

The ardent PTR advocates are few in number but they are extremely vocal and extremely influential. Let me provide just one example among many. Recently, I was watching a broadcast published in 2016 by Pastor John Hagee, a man for whom I have had great respect and with whom I agree with regarding so many things, particularly as those things relate to our relationship with the nation of Israel. However, in dealing with the rapture topic he was all over the map with myriad Scriptures that appeared, from the video, to leave people just nodding in uninformed agreement. I've heard and seen all this before but what followed was stunning. He said in a purposefully wimpish voice (i.e. about one-third the testosterone level of Pee Wee Herman), that some people say, "The church is going to go through the tribulation. Isn't that wonderful?" Having just created a straw man, Pastor Hagee then derisively responds to the alleged statement in a super-macho voice, "No meathead, that's not wonderful!" The implications were not subtle. To Pastor Hagee, people who believe in a post-trib rapture are apparently effeminate little weasels because that's how he portrayed them. He contrives a situation alleging that there are those who believe going through persecution is wonderful. I have never in my years, and I'm not that much younger than Pastor Hagee, ever heard anyone say it would be wonderful to go through the tribulation. But he has to set up the false premise to be able to retaliate. He has to have a fictional statement to rebuke and finishes it off with a derisive outburst of self-justified wrath. The way he made fun of other believers was beyond the pale. Maybe he thinks that believing in a post-trib rapture means you're not a Christian at all and therefore the ridicule is justifiable. I was very disappointed yet I continue to hold the man in very high regard.

Now, I have to be clear here for when I refer to PTR advocates and PTR apologists, I'm referring to those that *dominate* the discussion regarding the PTR. I'm not referring to the overwhelming number of people who subscribe to the PTR doctrine, both parishioners and pastors, who are godly and God-loving individuals and who with all sincerity have accepted this teaching in the ordinary course of listening to pastors' sermons or having learned it in a seminary. However, the importance of a proper understanding of end time events regarding the rapture is critical so as to not cause believers to stumble in these latter days when time and events prove their position to be unfounded.

Only those who have unfortunately embraced the PTR perspective run the risk of experiencing a faith-shaking wake-up call upon discovering that this "core" belief is false. The post-tribulationist on the other hand, if wrong in his doctrine, bears no risk or responsibility to himself or others. The reason is because no harm accompanies a potential error. If one believes that we will go through the great tribulation but instead is raptured beforehand, such a turn of events will not negatively impact that person's faith. On the contrary, he/she will be thrilled to have been wrong. None of this is to suggest, however, that one should abandon the PTR perspective simply for the purpose of hedging one's bets. This is only an observation but it happens to be true.

Even if the PTR position is correct, it still must be remembered that one does not enjoy its stated benefits simply because one believes in it. I once was told by a former pastor who could not convince me of the correctness of the PTR position, "Well, you can stay here if you want, but I'm getting out of here." While there are things that we don't receive if we don't believe, not believing that the rapture occurs prior to the tribulation does not render one "ineligible" to depart with others if the PTR position were correct.

While I have personally long abandoned the PTR position, my training as a lawyer causes me to continuously consider and reconsider the strengths of another party's position. There are biblical issues so clear from Scripture that the only debate that could arise is between believers and non-believers. But this isn't one of them. Rock-solid Christians are on both sides of this debate. But a critical point needs to be made, a point that applies even if the PTR position were correct.

Every time I have heard the PTR position advocated it is in essence proffered, more or less as follows: "While Christians may suffer some as things get darker, we won't have to go through the intensity of the tribulation because we will be raptured before it reaches a critical point." There is a monumental flaw in both the Scriptural understanding of events and I might add, logic, in this perspective.

To start, the context in which the PTR position is taught invariably assumes that the end of the United States means the end of the world as clearly exemplified by Pastor Hagee's message previously noted. It assumes that judgment on the United States means judgment simultaneously on the whole world. The teaching assumes that great tribulation of Christians in the United States cannot and will not occur apart from great tribulation everywhere else. It assumes that we, unlike those who have gone before us, will not suffer our own great tribulation for the sake of the Gospel due to apostasy unique to the United States. The truth of these assumptions is revealed in the zeal with which the PTR doctrine is rather uniquely preached in the US. If PTR apologists did not embrace these assumptions, then there would be no explanation for their zeal. Indeed, what would be the purpose for its intense advocacy?

By all accounts, those who endorse a PTR doctrine, as it relates to escaping tribulation in the United States, are likely in for a rude awakening. While Islam has for years painted the US as the "great Satan," they are actually much closer to being correct than they have ever been. The Obama administration took it upon itself to carry its message of abortion and aberrant sexual license throughout the whole world. Indeed, President Obama obsessed over all things homosexual in his crusade to not only fundamentally transform the United States, but to also fundamentally transform the entire world. While Islam certainly beats us in the "anti-Israel" department (though the Obama administration did its level best to catch up), the US clearly exceeds Islam in its advocacy for the freedom to execute innocent unborn human life and to declare, decree and impose sexual debauchery as the new global norm.

While there are certainly other countries that match the United States' proclivity (particularly under Obama) to support all things unbiblical, there is no other nation that has *advocated* for such evils worldwide. Without question, the United States' biggest export has become sin. And for a nation founded upon biblical principles (i.e., "to whom much is given, much is required"), there is probably not a single nation in the world presently more deserving of God's judgment than the United States.

So even if true, the way the PTR is taught does not accomplish any purpose of preparation for coming events. Preparation, one must ask, for what and for what purpose? There would be no reason for its urgent and incessant teaching but for the purpose of providing some assurance of protection from coming events to nervous congregations in the United States who see things going south at an alarming rate but want to feel "protected." But when the coming events of personal or national tribulation have nothing to do with the Great Tribulation, then where is the assurance? Indeed, what is the very purpose of the teaching? In fact, it has the unintended consequence of actually "un-preparing" people for tribulation ahead; tribulation that may be great and definitely will be personal but has no connection whatsoever to the Great Tribulation referenced in Scripture. In other words, just because the US is judged for its sins does not mean the beginning of the Great Tribulation is upon the world. It only means that like other nations in the past, the United States is being judged for *its* sins.

No one disputes that II Thessalonians 2:3-4 describes the revelation of the anti-Christ and with that revelation, the instigation of great worldwide tribulation and persecution. It says:

> "Let no man deceive you by any means: for that day shall not come except there come a falling away first, and that man of sin be revealed, the son of perdition." 31

Paraphrased, the return of the Lord won't precede the revealing of the anti-Christ. The anti-Christ can't persecute Christians or Jews openly of course until he is revealed. The anti-Christ won't be revealed until there is a great falling away (either immediately preceding or coincident with his revealing). But note what the Scripture does *not* say: "Let no man deceive you by any means: for that day shall not come except there first come a falling away *in the United States.*"

No place in Scripture is the downfall of the United States the trigger point for the revelation of the anti-Christ (which in turn triggers worldwide persecution). The moral, financial, military and spiritual implosion of the US has no biblical connection whatsoever to the beginning of the end times or the persecution referenced as part and parcel of the Great Tribulation. Specifically, the rapture is not an event primarily to catch away Christians in the United States before they have to suffer as others have (without a rapture) over several millennia. The United States can come under God's judgment for the same reasons as Israel and in the course of that judgment, we, as Christians in the United States, may have to give up our lives to our persecutors. We may certainly suffer as have other Christians over several millennia apart from any greater event of judgment even remotely approximating the Great Tribulation. In any case, God is not particularly America-centric. The United States is not the center of the world, especially His world.

I don't want to say that PTR apologists are elitist in their thinking or imply that they would contend that the end of the United States must mean that it's the beginning of the Great Tribulation. But the United States could slip into moral oblivion while other nations (China, South Korea, etc.) could be in a season of Christian ascendancy and blessing. In other words, the world may not be ripe yet for the revelation of the anti-Christ even though Christians in America are being slaughtered by ISIS, in prisons fighting rats off our earlobes, being beheaded and all those other things associated with persecution and tribulation that until this point in time have gone on elsewhere except in the United States.

It is elitist however; if one thinks we are above persecution and tribulation. Christians were executed in the first century. Armenian Christians were slaughtered in the early 20th century. Christians in Nazi Germany and Stalin's Russia were killed or imprisoned in WWII. There were Christian beheadings in Egypt in 2015. If one believes that beheadings can't happen in the United States without it being part of a grand end-times event, then one does have a truly elitist view of Christianity in the United States. The danger in the US is that PTR theology weaves the coming persecution of Christians in America uniquely with the state of Christianity around the world under an end time anti-Christ scenario from which we will have the privilege of exiting; a privilege unknown to the faithful before us. There is no connection. Nothing in

Scripture connects tribulation for Christians specifically in the United States with an E-ticket ride out of here. Nothing.

In the late 1940's, the Christian missionaries in pre-Mao China were taught a PTR perspective of end times. Then, Mao came into power and many were slaughtered, caught off guard and unprepared. Did some stumble because they weren't removed in their time of great tribulation? One can only wonder. If at any given time Christians can come under persecution and great tribulation for their faith and be tortured, imprisoned and/or executed, then does the teaching of a PTR theology really serve any meaningful purpose? Might it actually provide a unique disservice to the Body of Christ? Even if PTR teaching were correct, the imperative and imminent sense applied to its teaching could leave people totally unprepared for enduring *non end-times tribulation.* On the other hand, even if the post-tribulation rapture teaching were incorrect it would actually prepare people for what lies ahead because the tribulation that lies ahead may have nothing to do at all with end-times tribulation.

Why is the PTR position so well received? The answer is simple. Because who doesn't want to avoid persecution? Jesus made it clear in the Gospels that one of the reasons he was telling us what would happen to the saints in the last days was so that we wouldn't be surprised and caught off guard since that could derail our faith. None of that makes the idea of suffering any more palatable but it does mean that with proper warning the likelihood of enduring to the end is more assured. But to a nation that has never experienced tribulation and persecution, the idea of suffering simply is not very consumer friendly. In short, the popularity of the PTR is a reflection of that which we *want* to hear.

It is sometimes said the Great Tribulation will be a persecution like no other. While that is true, it may not be true entirely in the way we have interpreted "great." The tribulation is great in part because of its pervasiveness, not solely because the torture is necessarily more sinister or the blade of the guillotine duller than ones used in previous Christian and Jewish executions. Tribulation is always occurring *somewhere* in the world but until the Great Tribulation it will not occur *everywhere* in the world. That, in part is what makes it "great."

As noted, the pervasiveness and imperativeness associated with PTR teaching reveals that it is implicitly believed by its proponents that the state of Christian America is inseparable from the end-time anti-Christ tribulation scenario. If we come under a persecution like that of Richard Wurmbrand and face death, torture, starvation and all that Christians have suffered for two thousand years (having nothing to do with end-times Great Tribulation I might add), then where is the comfort provided by the PTR teaching? A PTR is irrelevant at least to the generation who "loved their lives not unto death" while undergoing their own tribulation.

The PTR teaching assumes that we in the United States will be gone before things get really bad in this country. This error will cause many to stumble. When ISIS or whoever comes for their head they will wonder why they are still here. Remember, we aren't talking The Great Tribulation (yet). We're just talking about normal century-to-century tribulation that has gone on forever. Will people say, "I thought we'd be gone before this happened!" What else might those souls then begin to doubt about Scripture? The PTR position ignores that we could be judged for this nation's sins and that we could suffer just as Israel was judged and suffered accordingly. Indeed as the Lord makes clear in Ezekiel 21:3, a nation could sin so badly that even the righteous are caught up in it and suffer with the wicked from the fallout of God's judgment. Or we could simply suffer for the sake of the Gospel as thousands have since the resurrection of Jesus. As I mentioned earlier, PTR teaching actually un-prepares us for tribulation from any and all sources.

The bottom line is this: the assumptions associated with the PTR teaching, even if true, may cause many to doubt or possibly fall because of the surprise discovery that their personal "great tribulation" has nothing to do with THE GREAT TRIBULATION. Just because we are one of the very few nations where Christians have not suffered persecution and tribulation for the sake of the Gospel, does not mean that God has carved out an exception for us. It's more likely that we haven't yet had an opportunity to actually prove just how much we love Him.

Remember those individuals referenced by the writer of the Book of Hebrews, those who were sawn in half? That is no compassionate, quick execution. No humane, painless lethal injections there. And there was no rapture either; nothing from which they were "privileged" to be airlifted. Just those who loved God and who are in glory having overcome by the blood of the Lamb, the word of their testimony and not loving their lives unto death. As noted in Acts 14:22, it is with *much* tribulation that one enters into the Kingdom of God.

Now, let's examine the scriptural evidence, if there be any, for a pre-tribulation rapture.

CHAPTER 3

EXAMINING THE "EVIDENCE" ONE EXHIBIT AT A TIME

In the following chapters, we will look at a host of scriptures put forth as evidentiary support for the PTR. Evidence can be compelling, meaning that no other reasonable explanation could exist for a proposition. On a lower level, evidence can be merely persuasive in that it's not compelling in and of itself but when combined with other "non-compelling" or persuasive evidence, circumstantially produces a probability of truth. Of course, when something is only "persuasive" then other explanations must be considered to help determine just what the evidence really indicates and just how persuasive it really is. If persuasive evidence is effectively countered or dismissed by virtue of proving equally reasonable (or more reasonable) inter-pretations, then the value of any such evidence is negated.

I must state at the beginning of this analysis that there is not a single Bible verse that is compelling in its support for the PTR. I have never heard a PTR supporter identify one verse that, by itself, unequivo-cally points to a PTR. There are certainly those who sincerely believe that certain verses could stand alone for the proposition of a PTR, but most of these verses aren't even persuasive since they are easily capable of reasonable alternative and frankly, more persuasive, explanations.

If one PTR verse summarily dealt with the matter, nothing else would be needed. But what do we see instead from PTR advocates? We see elaborate charts of verses with boxes and arrows going in different directions that more resemble an electronic schematic diagram for an Apollo space launch. The impact is impressive and people's responses are understandable. Some examples of their responses are as follows: "Certainly this person is an expert and must know what he is talking about." "It must be true if it's this complex." "Obviously these people have studied this to a degree that is way beyond me, so they must be correct. I will just take their word for it since they are the experts." I can't even tell you how many people I know that have simply surrendered the understanding of end-time events to a PTR assumption because of the complexities of the position.

I don't suggest that the convolution is intentional or offered with an intent to deceive or mislead. Far from it. And I will admit that the PTR position *appears* scholarly. All I can surmise, however, is that it's more likely a desperate attempt to arrive at a desired result—an assurance of a tribulation—free conclusion to life. To be fair, the great majority of people who embrace the PTR theory simply reflect what they have been taught in church, bible school or by use of the Scofield Bible. A few PTR apologists however, seem to have made a living out of misleading people, even if without an intent to mislead. Passages are taken out of context; interpretation moves away from the plain meaning of the text and Scripture gets reassembled in a very unnatural order.

In the PTR world, the interpretation of Scripture doesn't produce the result. Instead, the desired result produces the interpretation of Scripture. Starting with the conclusion, verses are interpreted through a PTR lens. The PTR analysis quite simply starts with the conclusion or an assumed truth of a PTR and from there the thought process works backwards through Scripture in an attempt to prove the merits of the PTR position. This is the result of starting with a pre-determined conclusion.

A prosecutor, in court, doesn't get to start with the conclusion that the accused is guilty. He can't say that because the defendant is guilty then this is how the evidence should be considered. Quite the contrary. The evidence to convict must proceed in a manner that when concluded leads a juror to only one result and that result is beyond a reasonable doubt. Anything less and the defendant walks. In short, the evidence must prove the conclusion. The conclusion can never prove the evidence.

In my 15 years of embracing a PTR perspective, quite unintentionally, I accumulated an inventory of troubling passages that incrementally raised my doubts regarding the scriptural viability of the PTR position. So I decided to do something very different. Out of raw determination, desperation and discipline, I managed to force myself to read the Bible starting with a conclusion; that being that the rapture occurs somewhere near the end of the tribulation. There was no other way to proceed given all of the troubling passages. In essence, I needed to adopt the PTR study method; that of starting with a conclusion so that I could now consider all those troubling passages from the other side of the fence. It was the only way by which I knew how to make progress knowing that any conclusion must still, ultimately be supported by the Word.

The result was startling. While a few new troubling passages appeared, an enormous number of previously troubling passages now made perfect sense. In short, while I wasn't breathing perfectly, there was a 90% improvement in air quality. At least the passages that now required a better understanding were manageable in number and were by no means daunting in substance. While I was still seeing through a "glass darkly", it was not nearly as dark as before and to this day continues to brighten as I pursue the truth.

Many passages will be considered throughout this book that will disprove a pre-tribulation rapture and establish with clarity a post-tribulation perspective but I want to provide at this juncture just one simple example of why a plain and chronological reading of Scripture compels a post-tribulation explanation of end time events. The Book of Zechariah is one of the most concise, chronological descriptions of end time events in all of Scripture. No one on either side of the debate will contend otherwise. The scripture references all of the nations being assembled against Jerusalem with Jesus, then returning by setting His feet upon the Mount of Olives, which is then split in two. It states in Zechariah 14:5 that all of the saints are with Him in that return. "All" means all. If the saints are raptured out of this world, 7 years earlier, then how can the saints who are saved during the tribulation (the PTR explanation for why there are so many saints on the earth during the tribulation) join Jesus in His return?

What is in view here can only be a post-tribulation event of bringing all the saints because this event is at the end of the tribulation. No one could reasonably contend that what is described in this chapter of Zechariah is a pre-tribulational event. For all those allegedly saved during the tribulation but who were not killed during the tribulation, how do they return on horses with the Lord when they don't even have glorified bodies yet? They haven't been killed and raised from the dead or raptured (remember, they missed the rapture) but they must join Jesus in His return because they are part of the "all saints" referenced in verse 5. And how about all the saints that are killed during the tribulation who obviously, by definition, missed the PTR? If "all" means "all" and I think it does, then they are with Jesus in this return as well but they need to be resurrected first. It would seem that the PTR theory would then necessitate yet another rapture to pick up this contingent of believers. Only a post-tribulation rapture occurring just before Jesus' return could logically explain how *all* of the saints get to join Him in that glorious return (without conflicting with other Scripture). More to the point, it doesn't require any convolution of Scripture or charts or graphs to get to this conclusion. It simply emerges from a plain reading of the text.

The verse by verse analysis which begins in the next chapter does not assume the importance of any one Scripture over another and as such, they are not set forth in any particular order. Different PTR apologists assemble them invariably in the order such apologists would deem to best demonstrate the strength of their proposition. The verses that will be discussed are those that are the heart and soul of the PTR doctrine. They represent the best evidence for a PTR; the ones that a PTR attorney would introduce as evidence. They are the passages that form the essential core of the doctrine as I have observed in the Statements of Belief in those churches where the PTR doctrine is part of that core. They are all of the verses that a PTR apologist would use in a debate. However, there will be some who will reach the end of this work and still ask the question, "Well how about this passage?" or "What about that passage?" The fact is that if the very best evidence for a PTR is dismissed, then there is little need to spend time on supplementary evidence since there is nothing to supplement. As you will see, the major problem with the PTR proof texts is that each is clearly capable of reasonable and often more probable interpretations in light of other Scripture indicating that there is *not* a PTR. If your evidence is equivocal, you really have no evidence at all.

To make the point another way, I have not left out of the analysis those Scriptures that I would use myself if I were assigned the task as part of a legal team to argue on *behalf* of a PTR. These are also the passages that have provided the greatest amount of confusion in the body of Christ. But in assessing their application, they require, if not demand, the purest intent and interpretation from the honest bible student who must proceed without preconceived notions.

CHAPTER 4

THE "RAPTURE" CHAPTER

The debate regarding the timing of the rapture begins with one particular passage of Scripture, I Thessalonians 4:13-18 (KJV) which states as follows:

> "But I would not have you to be ignorant, brethren, concerning them which are asleep (have died) that ye sorrow not, as others which have no hope. For if we believe that Jesus died and rose again, even so them also which sleep in Jesus will God bring with him. For this we say unto you by the word of the Lord, that we which are alive and remain unto the coming of the Lord shall not prevent them which are asleep. For the Lord himself shall descend from heaven, with a shout, with the voice of the archangel, and with the trump of God: and the dead in Christ shall rise first. Then we which are alive and remain shall be caught up together with them in the clouds, to meet the Lord in the air: and so shall we ever be with the Lord. Wherefore comfort one another with these words."

That this passage refers to the rapture is not in question by anyone who is a party to this case. Each side would admit this passage as evidence of the fact that a rapture will occur. So the issue is not if there will be a "catching away," but when. But a number of things should be noted.

First, this passage is remarkable when one considers the fact that had not the Thessalonians been concerned about the status of those Christians who had already passed away, this passage of Scripture wouldn't even exist. I don't want to suggest that its presence is somewhat casual or accidental. Obviously the Lord used the Thessalonians' concern as the basis upon which Paul felt compelled to address their concern while also introducing us to the fact that at a certain point in time, we exit. But its place in the Word certainly doesn't establish some major theological theme regarding a PTR and the context here makes that obvious. Timing of the rapture within the tribulation period is not discussed here.

Second, the comfort provided to the Thessalonians was to assure them that the dead in Christ would not be left behind or left out at Jesus' return. The "comfort" provided was not to give assurance to the Thessalonians that they wouldn't have to experience a Great Tribulation. The "comfort" referenced in this passage by PTR apologists is claimed to address a present day fear of having to endure great tribulation. But that application is misplaced as the text clearly demonstrates. 46

Third, while this passage clearly points to the existence of a rapture, it neither states nor even implies that it must occur prior to the tribulation. Nothing in this text remotely intimates a PTR. The way this passage is often presented is that once having proved that a rapture will occur (which it will), then presumptively it also proves <u>when</u> it will occur; i.e., before the tribulation starts. An evidentiary analogy would be as follows: that having proved the defendant happened to own a gun at the time of the alleged shooting, you have thereby proved that he actually used the gun in the commission of the crime. In law it's called a *non sequitur*, meaning, "it doesn't follow" or that what we have is a fundamental failure in logic. This passage can say no more than what it says, that there is a rapture in which the deceased Christians will be raised from the dead prior to those who are alive at the time and those who are alive at the time follow the deceased in short order. That is all.

Fourth, while this passage not only does not stand for the proposition of a PTR, if anything, it actually is evidence of the opposite, that is, that the rapture occurs at the end of the tribulation. Since the dead in Christ must rise first before those who are alive and remain can exit, logic demands a conclusion of a post-trib rapture. Why? If the Christian dead must rise before the living saints are raptured seven years before Jesus' return, then how can those that die after the PTR be raised up too? It seems that they have missed the boat. The obvious question relates to when do the dead in Christ arise? The answer is that they would rise at a resurrection.

However, Scripture only allows for two resurrections. The first one is that in which those who participate are blessed and includes those who are executed *during* the tribulation (as outlined in Revelation 20, it should go without saying that you can't be raised from the dead before you're dead). So, if it must include those that were killed during the tribulation, then the rapture can't occur before the dead who were to be raised in the rapture have died. And you don't want to be a part of the second resurrection (great white throne judgment).

This problem for PTR apologists is supposedly answered by breaking this first resurrection (of the saints) into two parts; phase one before the tribulation and phase two after the tribulation to raise all those Christians who died after the rapture during the tribulation. But wouldn't that at least admit a partial post-trib rapture? The claim is that this is all part of essentially one resurrection but with two parts. The problem is that there is absolutely zero evidence for a second *Christian* resurrection. This explanation of bifurcated or split raptures seven years apart exists solely because there is no other way to plug this gaping hole in the PTR doctrine. It is manufactured by man. Without it, it is the end of the road for a PTR but more on this when the entirety of Revelation 20:4-6 is discussed in a later chapter. The conclusion has dictated the evidence instead of the evidence dictating the conclusion.

Last, it is sometimes said that a PTR interpretation is appropriate for this passage from I Thessalonians because it fits with Romans 11:25 which states that "...blindness in part has happened to Israel until the fullness of the Gentiles be come in." It is appropriate only if the unjustified interpretation of one verse is to be explained by the unjustified interpretation of another. The argument is that while the Gospel is preached and received by Gentiles during a time of hardened Jewish hearts, Jewish hearts will be opened up when the Holy Spirit's move upon the Gentiles is done. I would generally agree. However, it also happens to quite nicely fit an assumption that the Holy Spirit is done and pulls up stakes in the Gentile world at the time of a PTR. That however, is pure speculation.

There are so many problems with using Romans 11:25 as a proof text of a PTR that it's difficult to know where to start but I will limit our discussion to two. First, the implication is that once the Gentile Christians are removed, only then can the Holy Spirit begin His work among the Jews. This ignores the obvious in that the Holy Spirit has never abandoned His work among the Jewish people. How else would one explain the growing number of Messianic Jews today? Even assuming the implication to be true for the sake of discussion, it still leaves a gaping hole in the PTR theory. Why? Because

Scripture does not indicate that a major work among the Jewish people begins simultaneously with the beginning of the tribulation. Indeed, the nation of Israel is still yet deceived well into the tribulation as the peace accord, struck with the anti-Christ, leads Israel to conclude that they have finally achieved a state of national tranquility.

Only when the abomination of desolation (three and one-half years into the tribulation) occurs does Israel finally get a clue that they were duped by the anti-Christ into a false peace treaty. In other words, the blinders for the nation of Israel appear to still be in place well into the tribulation. If the blinders are still on, is it not possible that the fullness of the Gentiles has not come in yet? And remember, we are now three and one-half years into the tribulation. Then there is a powerful evangelistic work among the nation of Israel. The timing is not precisely stated but it is certainly clear that it is not occurring for the first three and one-half years into the tribulation. Otherwise, Israel wouldn't have been deceived into believing they had achieved a lasting peace.

Second, Romans 11:25 could just as easily mean that the times of the Gentiles are not "come in" until the end of the tribulation and the rapture occurs at that time. Then and there God performs a quick work among the people of Israel such that "all Israel is saved" as the blinders have come off.

In conclusion, I Thessalonians 4:13-18 is clear evidence of the truth that a rapture will indeed occur but it says nothing regarding the timing of the occurrence prior to the tribulation. Neither this text nor the passage from Romans 11:25 provides any evidentiary support of anything regarding the possibility of a PTR. So using a text that proves only that a rapture will occur must come to a conclusion limited to that established fact. It provides no evidence of also establishing *when* the rapture will occur. If anything, these passages add credence to the proposition that the rapture occurs at the *end* of the tribulation. Any such support for a PTR here, exists solely by means of unilateral declaration, not by means of evidence within the passage itself or from without. And a jury would so find.

CHAPTER 5

I THESSALONIANS 5:9

"But let us, who are of the day, be sober, putting on the breastplate of faith and love: and for an helmet, the hope of salvation. For God hath not appointed us to wrath, <u>but</u> to obtain salvation by our Lord Jesus Christ." (I Thessalonians. 5:8-9 KJV).

One of the most often quoted scriptures in support of the PTR, the "God hath not appointed us to wrath" passage is also one of the most easily dismissed as evidence of a PTR. There are many reasons why this verse does not stand for the proposition for which it is so often proffered. As an introductory note, nothing in this passage or its context contains any reference to a rapture. The contrast being drawn by the Holy Spirit is between being appointed to heaven as opposed to being destined to hell. Paul is clearly addressing Christians. As Christians, our destiny is not a southbound freight but to complete our work in the course of our salvation. It's not God's desire that we incur His wrath as non-believers but rather His grace as believers. In short, He has appointed those who love Him to heaven and those who do not, to judgment.

The Lord is not making a reference to an escape scenario and there is nothing in the text that even remotely suggests that a rapture (at any time, pre-trib or post-trib, for that matter) is part of this discussion. Indeed, this passage clearly sets forth a simple contrast of opposites, "wrath" (hell) and "salvation" (heaven). It says, "not appointed to wrath <u>but</u> to obtain salvation." This passage does not say that there is a distinction between those who qualify for the rapture and those who don't. The contrast is between those appointed to heaven and those who aren't.

It seems that frequently the PTR advocates do not distinguish between tribulation and wrath. In fact, their use of this passage as text supportive of the PTR, necessitates that such advocates equate tribulation with wrath. If "not being appointed to wrath" means we get to exit before the Great Tribulation, then obviously the PTR advocates have equated "wrath" with "tribulation." Nothing could be further from the truth. "Tribulation" is mentioned 22 times in Scripture and never in the context of a rapture. "Wrath" is mentioned many times but <u>never</u> in the context of tribulation. The reason is simple. Tribulation and wrath are two entirely different events and originate from two entirely different sources. Tribulation is what Satan applies to the righteous and wrath is what God applies to the unrighteous (at His appointed times). Of course God has not appointed His wrath upon the righteous; that is reserved for the unjust. But tribulation is Satan's *modus operandi.* Matthew 13:21, states that "persecution arises for the word's sake. Jesus defeated Satan in the wilderness with the Word. Since, we, as believers have access to the same "tools" if you will, as Jesus, Satan is focused upon causing the greatest problems among those who can actually use that sword (the Word) against him.

Acts 14:22 reveals that it is through *much* tribulation that we enter into the Kingdom of God. Notice that the passage does not say that it is through much *wrath* that we enter into the Kingdom of God. This distinction is critical since the conflation of these two terms is a cause of great confusion.

The difference in the two terms is as significant as the difference between heaven and hell. We have a promise that God will never leave us nor forsake us and who promises rest upon every believer while in tribulation since the source of the tribulation is from none other than the enemy of our souls, Satan. Wrath though, is judgment against unbelievers and God does not provide comfort for those incurring His wrath. God would not supply the person marked for judgment with spiritual nourishment and grace at the same time that He visits His wrath upon them. And so, I Thessalonians 5:9 does not say that God has not appointed us unto tribulation. It is wrath we have not been appointed to. From Matthew 24 we know that it is in the middle of the Great Tribulation that the anti-Christ carries out the abomination of desolation and his identity is thereby revealed to Israel. It is not in the middle of the "Great Wrath."

The most obvious consequence of the misapplication of I Thessalonians 5:9 in support of a PTR is the unwitting imposition of stark contradictions into Scripture. While "not being appointed to wrath" presumptively means a ticket out of here via the rapture when the tribulation breaks forth, a question then arises regarding the status of all the post-tribulation saints. There are many Christians on earth during the Great Tribulation (presumed by PTR apologists to be those who accepted the Lord subsequent to the rapture). Whatever their origin, the fact that there are Christians on earth during the Great Tribulation is not in dispute. Are they simply the body of Christ existing on the earth at the beginning of the tribulation period (because there is no PTR) or are they, as the PTR apologists state, those who were "saved" subsequent to a PTR?

In no way can I Thessalonians 5:9 support the proposition that these are all saints who were saved after the rapture. To contend so would make God a liar. If the very reason that this passage supposedly supports a PTR position, that is, that God would not have His children go through the tribulation, then why would

His children who are saved *after* the rapture have to go through the tribulation? Why wouldn't this same passage of Scripture that would exempt the PTR saints also exempt the tribulation saints as well? Who are these tribulation saints that the Word now does not apply to them also? Why does God, who is the same, yesterday, today and forever and whose Word *is* forever settled in heaven now change the rules and His Word? Why has He become a "respecter of persons" contrary to all Scripture and why does He deviate from His Word and deny the same benefits of His immutable Word to those who got saved on the wrong side of the rapture fence?

The answer of course, is that God has not changed and tribulation saints are not second-class saints. Why? To begin with, they aren't tribulation saints. They are just saints in the tribulation enjoying all of the benefits of God's Word as every other group of believers throughout history who went through tribulation. They have not missed out on anything. There is no difference between these two groups of saints because there are not two groups of saints. Stated differently, there is no difference because there is no PTR to create such a difference. A person cannot create this false dichotomy without introducing contradictions in the Word. Only a post-tribulation rapture avoids the inevitable contradiction of having God say one thing to one group of people (PTR saints) and then withdraw the application of His Word from another group (tribulation saints). The PTR explanation imposes this irresolvable contradiction into the Word. Since the Word cannot contradict itself, then the theory that forces the contradiction needs to go. The PTR apologists must say that the saints on earth during the tribulation are those who were born again after the rapture. But they aren't tribulation saints because of proof. They're tribulation saints because PTR apologists declare them to be so otherwise, the PTR theory is shipwreck. But the shipwreck occurs nonetheless. In forming the distinction between the PTR and tribulational saints, this unwitting contradiction is then imposed into Scripture. That contradiction is that the PTR saints have the privilege of enjoying a benefit contained in the Word (not being appointed to wrath), but for some unexplainable reason, God's otherwise immutable Word doesn't apply to the tribulation saints.

The PTR doctrine unwittingly treats tribulation saints as chopped liver. Consider the contradiction introduced into God's word: the alleged saints who haven't undergone persecution get to leave early and the ones who, you could say, deserve to leave early because of what they have gone through don't get to leave.

A disclaimer must precede the final point of this chapter. I will not tell you that I know exactly when the rapture occurs. I do not know if we have arrived at that point in time that we need to know. With that disclaimer out of the way, it is scripturally possible that Christians could be here even during <u>some</u> of God's pouring out of His wrath upon the earth. Do I believe that? I do not know but I do not see Scripture necessarily precluding that possibility and here is why. When it states that God will pour His wrath out upon the inhabitants of the earth (Revelation 16), the PTR apologists state that this act by itself means no Christians could possibly be on earth at that time because again, we have not been appointed to wrath. But this conclusion short-changes the power and precision of our Creator.

It is clear that Christians are removed before the last, great and consummate act of wrath as set forth in Matthew 24 because Revelation 19 points out that we return with Him for the battle of Armageddon and Armageddon is part of His judgment. There are insights and clues provided in the Word, however, that we could be here during some of God's wrath albeit protected. In other words, we could be here for part of it but not be subject to it. This is not a possibility that Scripture prohibits. The fact is that God has no doubt exercised other acts of judgment upon peoples and nations during which time His people were present and preserved.

Many people will survive God's outpouring of wrath at the time of the Lord's return because His judgment deals primarily with the armies that oppose Israel at Armageddon. Many unbelievers who are not part of the anti-Christ's armies survive the great battle because they aren't part of that battle. Indeed, the nonbelievers on earth during the millennial reign of Christ must come from somewhere. But the contention that Christians could not be on earth during any out-pouring of any wrath would, frankly, indicate a belief that God is somehow not able to protect His own in the course of executing judgment on others.

This would be a low view of our Creator's strength and capability and almost ascribes to Him limitations associated with humanity—those things that humans can and cannot do. In this scenario, apparently God is not capable of executing wrath upon the earth without effecting collateral damage upon Christians. God may be the Creator but apparently He is incapable of carry-ing out judgment without there simultaneously being Christian casualties that stem from friendly fire.

Many passages prove this point of supernatural protec-tion of His own while judging others but I will settle upon only a few. The angel of death went through the camps in Egypt executing judgment upon all those who did not have the blood of the Passover lamb upon their doorposts. Was not the angel able to discern on the spot, while passing by, just who should be spared and who should not? Was there a requirement that the Hebrews be physically removed so that the angel would make no mistakes and strike the wrong party? God was able to implement a precise surgical judgment that did no harm to those to whom no harm should be done. He is God.

The judgment against the first born of Egypt was, of course, the climax to a series of judgments God poured out upon the Egyptians. While the impact of the first three of the plagues were evident among both the Hebrews and the Egyptians, it states in Exodus Chapter 8 that the day came when God would make a difference between the Hebrews and Egyptians and from that day forward the plagues in Egypt had no impact upon the Hebrews. God was more than able to protect His own from judgment while in the process of inflicting widespread judgment against others.

Numbers 16 tells the story of Korah's rebellion when 250-plus men, moved by jealousy and envy, challenged Moses' authority in the wilderness. While the Lord told Moses to tell the people to separate themselves from the rebels, in no way did the separation reflect an admission by God that He could not selectively strike the guilty parties without inflicting "civilian casualties." God was about to perform a very different kind of execution as He opened up the earth and the earth swallowed the faction and all their goods upon which the earth then closed. The impact of this type of execution/wrath had its intended impact upon the others who were not caught up in the rebellion. God was not incapable of a surgical judgment upon each of the guilty parties without having to separate the offenders from the innocent. Instead the separation was necessary only because of the *type* of judgment He chose to impose. It was simply the first "ground-breaking" ceremony of its kind.

In Acts 5:1-11 the story is told of two half-hearted disciples by the names of Ananias and Sapphira. The two of them, husband and wife, participated in a lie to the Holy Spirit, even though each of them committed the offense independent of the other. The result was that God slew each of them on the spot at the telling of their lie. No collateral damage. No one nearby was hurt accidentally. God simply judged them in a manner not exactly described in Scripture but from which it is clear that others were within what could have only been several feet of each of them. God's wrath was visited upon them with great exactness. It couldn't have been more precise. He is God.

Chapters 8 and 9 in the Book of Revelation describe in succession the sounding of trumpets by angels where at the blowing of each trumpet, a different judgment upon the earth is unleashed. Whether it is one-third of the trees being destroyed, one-third of the sea being turned into blood or one-third of the drinking waters of earth being made poisonous (along with a host of other "one-third" judgments), a point always overlooked is that two-thirds of the trees will not be destroyed, two-thirds of the sea will not be turned into blood nor will two-thirds of the drinking water be made poisonous. Why do these judgments only touch one-third of the various elements referenced in this passage? Would it be mere speculation to say that it is possible that there are "believers" still on the earth and that God would prevent them from being directly impacted by these judgments? Is it possible that there are those for whom trees and good drinking water is preserved? Is it possible that one household could turn on their faucet and get blood out of the tap or poisonous water while a neighbor is drinking water as pure as the angel provided Elijah in I Kings 19? Revelation 9:3-4 answers these questions in part since when locusts with the sting of scorpions are loosed upon the earth, the locusts are commanded to hurt "only those men which have not the seal of God in their foreheads." Obviously, there are those upon the earth caught up in the middle of judgment but who themselves incur no wrath from God.

The simple point is that God can and does preserve his own while judging those who are not His own. As with Noah's family, these men are not removed or raptured during or from this judgment. Rather they are once again spared in *the midst* of judgment. Once again, God does not provide an exit; He provides protection. Remember, He is God.

As I stated at the beginning of the discussion of this point of preservation in the midst of judgment, I do not know exactly when and where at the end of the tribulation we get to leave. But the PTR apologists clearly state that believers cannot be here during any of the tribulation that they confuse with the out-pouring of God's wrath. The point is not that believers are here during any of God's judgment, but simply that they could be. I don't know and this is not an attempt to make that case; however, God is able to protect us in the midst of His wrath if He so chose. Believers are certainly here during the tribulation since "wrath" and "tribulation" are not interchangeable terms and have nothing to do with each other as previously noted. Ironically, we are around for the last act of Judgment. That's when we get to ride on white horses with Jesus' return as part of His posse.

I Thessalonians, 5:9 is a wonderful passage of Scripture but as we have seen for a host of reasons, it does not have the meaning given to it by the PTR apologists; a meaning not supportable from the context, by reason or by other Scripture. The case for a pre-tribulation rapture citing this verse as evidence is not just weak; it is non-existent.

CHAPTER 6

THE REVELATION 3:10 CONUNDRUM

In Revelation 3:10, Jesus speaking to the church of Philadelphia states,

> "Because you have kept My command to persevere, I also will keep you from the hour of trial which shall come upon the whole world, to test those who dwell on the earth." New King James Version (NKJV)

The King James Version uses the phrase, "Because thou hast kept the *word of my patience*" which the NKJV translates as "persevere." For the sake of efficiency in this discussion, I will use the term "persevere" instead of "word of my patience."

One should note Jesus' use of the word "hour" of trial or testing referenced in this verse. Students of eschatology make frequent reference to Daniel's "seventieth week" to identify the seven year period of tribulation prior to which (according to PTR apologetics) Christians are raptured. A "week" is seven years, making a "day" one year. Interestingly, this passage does not say that He will keep us from the week of trial or testing, or even the day of trial or testing, but only the hour of trial or testing. I don't want to go too far with this point or become dogmatic, but the mathematical equivalent of an "hour", if using the word "week" denotes seven years, is only about 2 weeks. In other words, while the tribulation is three and a half years in its most intense form, the actual time of God's testing the earth (i.e., wrath), may in any event, be remarkably short. Since we've already established that wrath and tribulation are not the same because they have different authors, it should come as no surprise that they would not be of the same length either. There is no reason that they should be.

The hot button discussion from this passage is what does the word "from" mean in the phrase, "will keep you from the hour…?" To quote Steve Hall and his research from Aboundingjoy.com:

> "The preposition 'from' (Greek: *ek*) implies direction ('out from within'). It is *not* a synonym for 'away from in some other place.' This implies that the church is within the hour of testing and is to be kept or guarded from danger. In heaven there would be no danger to be 'kept' from. The Greek for 'keep' is 'tehreo' which implies 'to keep from a present danger.'

The only other New Testament verse which uses both words is John 17:15, where it is very clear that removal is not implied. Similar ideas are expressed when Jesus used the words, 'Father save me <u>from</u> this hour,' or when we pray, 'Deliver me <u>from</u> this time of sickness.' We do not mean, 'Rapture me out of the world!'

For example John 17:15 says, 'I pray <u>not </u>that thou shouldest take them out of the world, but that thou shouldest <u>keep</u> them <u>from</u> the evil.' 'Now is my soul troubled; and what shall I say? Father, save me <u>from</u> this hour: but for this cause came I unto this hour.' (John 12:27) 'Alas! for that day is great, so that none is like it: it is even the time of Jacob's trouble; <u>but he shall be saved out of it</u>'. (Jeremiah 30:7) Note that John 17:15 and Revelation 3:10 use the same Greek words for 'keep' and 'from'. God will preserve him in the midst of the trouble and bring him through it.

PTR advocates would contend a different meaning to the word "from," however, at best, it is an equivocal interpretation. Equivocal evidence is the same as no evidence. Besides, when you consider other passages in Jesus' discourse on the seven churches of Revelation, the PTR interpretation of the word "from" is even less tenable. For example, the cited passage relates to the church in Philadelphia that is considered the "faithful" church but another one of the so-called "good" or honorable churches described in Revelation 2 and 3 is the church at Smyrna, also known as the "persecuted" church.

It states in Revelation 2:10 (NKJV) with respect to the church at Smyrna:

> "Do not fear any of these things which you are about to suffer. Indeed the devil is about to throw some of you into prison that you may be tested and you will have tribulation ten days. Be faithful until death and I will give you the crown of life."

So the obvious question is why are the saints in Smyrna imprisoned and then apparently executed with no opportunity to escape by rapture but according to PTR doctrine the saints in the church of Philadelphia get to escape before things get really bad? We have the very same problems as we had in the previous chapter dealing with "not being appointed unto wrath" applying to PTR saints but supposedly the tribulation saints" must lose their heads. Why is God also in this section of Scripture applying different rules to different saints and becoming a respecter of persons? Does God have favorites? God forbid. This application of Scripture to a PTR again forces a serious contradiction into the Word. The saints in Smyrna cannot be on the chopping block while the saints in Philadelphia get a quick exit, that is, not without making God a liar.

The PTR advocates' answers to this dilemma are varied but starting with a conclusion, they find a way to interpret backwards through this section of Scripture to fit their conclusion. The explanation I have heard the most is that these two churches existed at different times and that the church in Smyrna represents a church age that has passed. This is part and parcel of the "dispensational approach" to Scripture. However, the churches in Revelation absolutely bear no chronology in time. They simply represent seven different churches, all of which existed at the time of John's writing of Revelation but also represent the entire spectrum of churches today and throughout the ages. There have always been churches (and still are) that are compromising, corrupt, faithful, persecuted, loveless, lukewarm and dead. These are the seven different churches described in Revelation and I can tell you personally that I think I have visited at least five of them. But to say that each church predominated in a particular age and then ceased, only to give way to another dominant church is devoid of all biblical support.

To say that the persecuted church is of a past age would be an insult to all those brothers and sisters throughout the world who, even as I write, are undergoing intense and immense persecution. This supposed chronology is without any biblical support but

PTR apologists have walked their own plank by suggesting such a chronology that places the church in Philadelphia at the end of the church age.

That is because the last church in the chronology set forth in Revelation, however, is not the church in Philadelphia but the church of Laodicea, also known as the "lukewarm" church. If that is the last church and the last church is, by definition, the final church existing at the time of the last days, then that means that the church age of the church in Philadelphia has passed also and the verse that would qualify people for escape via the rapture has passed us by as well. If we are going to get out of here early, then we needed to leave in a previous church age. But a previous church age would not be close to the end times from which the rapture is supposed to deliver us. Do you see the mess this creates? The suit, no matter how tailored, doesn't fit. There is neither logic nor a biblical basis for the claim that this passage supports a PTR. But that is not all.

If at this point of the chapter you still have your doubts (I know, the PTR hold is a strong one because it is what we want to believe), then you must deal with the Revelation 3:10 conundrum. Without question, the pervasive and consistent teaching of the PTR relates directly to the intent and desire to assure Christians that they will not face a time of intense persecution for their faith. If that were not the intent, then what would be the purpose for all the time spent on teaching it anyway? It is to calm souls in the face of the anxiety otherwise associated with anticipated suffering during the Great Tribulation.

The fundamental problem is that this passage, ignoring everything else in this chapter, still does not say what PTR advocates say it says or want it to say. That is because the reference in the passage is not to Christians as a whole but only to those who "persevere." Do you know any Christians that appear to not be persevering? How about 50, 60 or 70%? Are these not actually the ones referenced in some of the 7 churches described in Revelation, ones who are dead, or loveless or compromising or lukewarm? We are not to judge but we know they exist and likely in large numbers.

So this is the conundrum. How does a passage that is taught as an assurance that if you are a Christian, you will be spared from end-time tribulation provide that assurance when, by the limitation set forth in the passage itself, a large number of those relying on this false comfort will be disqualified because they are one of the many Christians who aren't persevering? Some comfort. How do you achieve a place of knowing that you have in fact persevered and that you are now "in the club?" How do you know that having been admitted to the club that you have not since been excommunicated because you are not persevering like you used to persevere? These may seem like foolish questions but the reason behind the PTR teaching actually renders these questions legitimate.

So the logical question becomes, if Revelation 3:10 does not have application to a PTR, then just what does it mean and how is it distinguishable from the church at Smyrna where the saints have to give it up? There are two possible explanations and both are viable. Their application is the same but involves two slightly different scenarios. First, it may be that God protects the "Philadelphia saints" from His trying/ testing of the inhabitants of the earth. In other words, we may be back to the difference between tribulation and wrath. The issue with those of the church in Smyrna is not God's wrath. They are victims of Satan's wrath (i.e. tribulation). Revelation 2:10 even references tribulation from the devil, not wrath of God upon the ungodly. Those who persevere in Philadelphia are not appointed unto God's wrath but the saints who are persecuted in Smyrna; those who undergo tribulation (Satan's wrath) because Jesus promised that we would; those are the ones who have washed their robes in the blood of the lamb. (Rev 7:14).

As you can see, the failure to distinguish between God's wrath and Satan's tribulation continues to course through the entire PTR theory. It may not have seemed very consequential at the onset but the error metastasizes and affects one's view of end time events in many ways. It is as if one could shoot at the moon with a 22-caliber rifle and when you aim, you are off by a mere one degree. However, several hundred thousand miles out, that seemingly minor error in trajectory results in missing the moon by four thousand miles. After all, when you make a wrong turn, the farther you go in the wrong direction it should be no surprise that you are farther from your destination.

The second possible explanation is that the saints, while in the very heat of tribulation, are kept from taking the mark of the beast. In other words, because the saints have persevered, God will provide a way of escape for them to not worship the beast or take the mark. Of course, the likely result for not taking the mark is that the one refusing is simply executed. The result then is the same as for the Christians of Smyrna. They will be executed but the difference in the two possible explanations boils down to this. Under scenario one, the Christians who have persevered are protected from that which God is bringing upon the earth. In the second scenario, they are provided a way of escape from the situation of being forced to take the mark of the beast while enduring Satan's tribulation. Either could be true. The result for our purposes is the same. This passage does not, in any event, exempt Christians from going through the Great Tribulation. Those who persevere are either provided a way of being able to escape the mark of the beast or their perseverance is rewarded with supernatural exemption during the earlier phases of God's wrath.

This concept of "preservation in the midst of" or "protection without removal" shows up in other places in Scripture as well. One example comes from Zephaniah 2:3 where it states "Seek ye the Lord, all ye meek of the earth, which have wrought this judgment; seek righteousness, seek meekness: it may be ye shall be *hid* in the day of the Lord's anger." Notice the emphasis on "hid" as an "escape in place" since removal is not in the context as in being "physically removed."

Another example is John 17:15 in which Jesus is praying for his disciples and, as previously noted, asks the Father not to take the disciples out of this world but to protect them from persecution and evil and to do so in place. The PTR retort to this verse is that it only has application to Jesus' disciples at that point in time; that Jesus knew what they would soon have to endure and that He doesn't reach forward in his application to the end times. The problem with that conclusion is that the passage itself refutes that application for in verse 20 Jesus makes it clear that He is not only praying this prayer for His "current" disciples but for all those who would believe thereafter. In other words, Jesus' prayer to not remove His own, but for His own to be protected in the midst of tribulation, reaches all the way to the end of the age.

Without question though, it is bad news as you might expect, if someone doesn't persevere. Hebrews 10:39

warns us of the consequences of falling back into or shrinking back into perdition. Compromise will be to the destruction of our soul. If those who persevere escape God's wrath, does it not conversely imply that those Christians who don't persevere are in some way affected by God's wrath? One need only review the warnings given by Jesus to the churches in Revelation 2 and 3 to come up with the obvious answer. Just maybe we now know what the passage really means when it says that we are to "work out our salvation with fear and trembling."

But to the point of this chapter and book, the use of the passage under consideration in this chapter as a proof text for a PTR fails the evidentiary requirements to prove a PTR. The alternative explanations that we have explored negate any evidentiary value this passage otherwise has in attempting to prove a PTR. And both alternative explanations point to the truth of a post-tribulation rapture. Again, equivocal evidence for a PTR is no evidence at all.

One final comment is in order. It states in Matthew 24 that those who endure to the end will be saved. The converse, of course, is that those who do not persevere until the end will not be saved as previously referenced in this chapter. It is clear that enduring (also persevering) does not apply until things start to get rough. After all, what is involved in enduring easy times? What is the need to persevere if you do not suffer from tribulation and persecution? To only endure up to the point of a PTR is not endurance at all if you exit just when the tough sledding begins. The PTR theory renders this passage from Matthew 24 hollow, if not meaningless. More on Matthew 24 later, but now let us move on to the last of the PTR theory pillars, Luke 21:36.

CHAPTER 7

EXIT STAGE RIGHT?

The PTR position is essentially a three-legged stool. The first two we have discussed in the previous two chapters, I Thessalonians 5:9 and Revelation 3:10. The last leg of the stool is Luke 21:36 (KJV) which states:

> "Watch ye therefore, and pray always, that ye may be accounted worthy to <u>escape</u> all these things that shall come to pass, and to stand before the Son of Man."

Chapter 21 of Luke is a parallel passage of Scripture with Matthew 24 but this verse is missing from Matthew 24. The word to note is "escape."

The first thing to consider is the meaning of "all these things." This discourse begins in verse 6 where Jesus describes the things that will come upon the earth including wars, earthquakes, famines and pestilence along with signs and fearful wonders occurring in the heavens. Jesus then makes the point in verse 12 that other things must happen before we get to the *grand finale.*

He states that they will be hated for His name; they will be imprisoned, betrayed by friends and family and some will be executed. Luke 21: 18-19 makes a remarkable statement that they should not worry (but be patient) because not even a hair on their heads would perish or be lost. I raise verse 18 only because the passage cannot be in reference to a PTR (that is, that no hairs on your head perish because you've been whisked away in a PTR). Verse 18 has nothing to do with being raptured to avoid tribulation. Why? Because Jesus just got done saying that some of them would receive the death penalty. Obviously it means some-thing else that does not contradict the very plain meaning of Luke 21:16 regarding the execution of some saints.

So, how do you reconcile Jesus' statement that "Not a hair on your head" would be lost with the comment that "some of you shall they cause to be put to death?" They are not contradictory. In Matthew 10:30 Jesus made the comment that even the hairs on people's heads are numbered and hence known to God. This proves that God knows everything and He cares about us right down to the most minute detail, namely, the number of hairs on our head. His comment in Luke 21: 18 and 19 would accurately be paraphrased as, "Do not worry, nothing will escape My notice." He has things in control but "in control" just happens to include some Christians being executed for His glory according to their faith. Don't worry. Their honor will match their faithfulness.

But Jesus follows with a description of events that clearly reveals that the discourse up to that point regards events that, while prospective at the time, are in our rear view mirror now. The reference is to the destruction of Jerusalem that led to the scattering of the Jews throughout the world. So when Jesus said, "Before all these things" (tribulation events) some other things must happen first, He was projecting a fairly short distance down the road to the scattering of the Jews that occurred in approximately 70 A.D.

The parallel passage in Matthew 24 is an end-time reference as it is set in the context of following the abomination of desolation and makes clear reference to the Great Tribulation (Matthew 24:21). Because there can be no conflict in Scripture, then Jesus is speaking one prophecy (in Matthew and Luke) that accurately describes two events for two different times. This is frequent in Scripture such as the prophetic statements from David that had application in the near term to David but also much later to Jesus. Psalm 22 is an example. So while the context of Luke 21:36 is a reference to the destruction of Jerusalem in 70 A.D., He is also describing the identical challenge of the saints at the last days in Matthew.

Jesus continues the discourse in Luke 21 in an exclusively end-time context that could only refer to the very last of the last days as follows:

> 25 "And there shall be in the sun, in the moon, and in the stars: and upon the earth distress of nations with perplexity; the sea and the waves roaring:
>
> 26 Men's hearts failing them for fear, and for looking after those things which are coming on the earth: for the powers of heaven shall be shaken.
>
> 27 and then they shall see the Son of man coming in a cloud with power and great glory.
>
> 28 And when these things begin to come to pass, then look up, and lift up your heads; for your redemption draweth nigh."

This passage points to a number of things. First, it is clear from all these verses that we are definitely in the very end of times. Next, it is not coincidental that Jesus comes in the clouds (the same place we meet him in the rapture described in I Thessalonians 4:17). The rapture reference is the statement in verse 28 "to look up." That would mean that the rapture is an event occurring just prior to Jesus' return when we meet in the clouds (our redemption draws nigh). It also should be noted that it doesn't come as a complete surprise either. Finally and to further underscore the previous point, it is clear that there are Christians on earth at the very last of days because they are the ones looking for their redemption. The lost certainly won't be on the lookout for the Savior.

PTR apologists attempt to deal with this thorny issue by declaring that this does not apply to Christians, having long since been raptured. The proposition is that these are not Christians being referenced but Jews because Jesus' audience was Jewish. The text does not support that conclusion.

If you start with the assumption that the PTR is the only available interpretation for end-time events, then the interpretation of Scripture is forced to fit that assumption. One way or another the suit must be made to fit. An analogy from law would be in order. In court, a proper presentation of the evidence would be, "because of Exhibits A through J and other evidence, it is clear that the defendant is guilty." PTR reasoning is "because the defendant is guilty, then this is how you should interpret Exhibits A through J." It should be a Scripture-based conclusion, not a conclusion-based interpretation of Scripture.

There is a bit of sophistry as well in the assertion that because only Jews are being addressed, the application of Jesus' discourse is necessarily limited to the Jews. It would be as though the coach of the Detroit Lions said to the team at half-time, "The only way we can win is by playing hard all 60 minutes.

Nothing less than a full and committed effort will win this ball game!" Would one conclude that because the coach was talking to the Detroit Lions' team that such otherwise universal advice only had application to the Lions? Would it not apply to all teams similarly situated? The fact is that every speech has its immediate audience but it is illogical to conclude that the application of a topic must be limited to the audience receiving the instruction. In fact, by this same reasoning, the Sermon on the Mount then has no application to Gentile believers because Jesus' audience was Jewish. By this reasoning, Gentile Christians should forget about 98% of everything Jesus personally said because Jesus was only addressing Jews at that time of speaking.

Luke 21:31 makes it clear that Christians are on the earth because who else present at that time would know to watch and look for these things to happen with the knowledge that it meant that the Kingdom of Heaven was close at hand? Not unbelievers. All of which, now brings us to verse 36. What does it mean? Specifically, what does "escape" mean in the context of this verse?

It is assumed by PTR advocates that this means to be removed "from" as in to another location. It is the very same analysis to which we subjected Revelation 3:10 in the previous chapter. However, the same word is used in I Corinthians 10:13 wherein it states:

"There hath no temptation (or test) taken you but such as is common to man but God is faithful, Who will not suffer you to be tempted above that ye are able; but will with the temptation also make a way to *escape*, that ye may be able to *bear* it."

"Bear" is the same as endure. The believer does not escape by being whisked away from the situation but rather God provides a way to bear it or endure it. Again, as with Revelation 3:10, it is escape or deliverance in the midst of the challenge not apart from the challenge. After all, God said to Paul "my grace is sufficient for you." But did God extricate Paul physically? And sufficient for what? It is sufficient to bear anything and everything because of His grace.

The key to understanding this passage goes all the way back to the beginning of this discourse. Jesus made clear reference to what the saints would go through leading up to the destruction of Jerusalem in 70 A.D. which is also, as stated, a foreshadowing of what saints would go through later. But in any event, consider their plight. First, saints are dragged before their accusers, which God allows, since it is an opportunity for them to testify. When you consider it, is it not one of the only ways to witness to a lost judge, jury, bailiff or even higher rulers, even if the opportunity requires that you be unjustifiably arrested? That's what Paul learned.

Second, this passage makes it clear that everyone will hate them because of the name Yeshua to which they are inextricably linked. This alone reveals that the real offense is being a Christian, not necessarily a Jew. Next, comes betrayal at the hands of friends and family. Imagine being betrayed by your mother, your husband or children just for being a Christian. This is followed by execution for some, for the same crime that Richard Wurmbrand committed, publicly declaring the Gospel of Jesus Christ. Sounds like tribulation to me. Is there anything Jesus left out? I suppose you could say that Jesus did not specifically mention torture but being "dragged" before your accusers does not exactly imply that the accused is enjoying all of his constitutional rights.

Further, Jesus makes a specific reference to extreme tribulation relating to a time period that has no relationship to end times tribulation. This is enormously significant. As a precursor to the experience of the saints in the last days, He is showing that what will happen in the end will have happened before (extreme tribulation in 70 A.D.) and what will have happened before is no different than what will happen to the saints in the end. This is one of the gold nuggets of Luke 21.

Verse 36 should rock everyone to their core. The issues of whether "escape" means to be removed as in extricated physically or to be given supernatural protection in place has been resolved. However, for the sake of showing just how sobering this passage is, I will, for the sake of discussion, let "escape" mean being physically removed. In other words, I will let the PTR advocates have their definition. Warning: The following is not for the faint of heart.

Only those "watching" and "praying always" are eligible to be counted worthy of "escaping." How can this verse mean all Christians when not all Christians are watching and praying always? Or does this imply that the road really is narrow and that one is not a Christian if you are not always watching and praying?

PTR apologists can't have it both ways. You can't go to this verse and say that anyone who has supposedly made a confession of Jesus Christ as Lord is saved and will avoid the tribulation if they aren't praying and watching always. The dilemma created by the PTR doctrine is twofold. Either, it must suppose two classes of Christians; the vigilant and diligent who get to leave early and the sluggards who do not. Or alternatively, authentic Christians are a rather "select" group that has satisfied qualifications much higher than we normally "require" to be considered "Christian." Put bluntly, the alternative is that the sluggards aren't even Christians.

Therefore, the following are fair questions. Are there Christians being referenced in Luke 21:34 who are carousing and caught up with the cares of the world that do not get raptured along with the rest of the church? Are all those who watch and pray a smaller group than the entire church that the PTR advocates contend exit by virtue of this verse? Does working out our salvation with fear and trembling mean watching and praying always? Does a supposed confession of faith in fifth grade or a foxhole conversion in the war followed by a life of careless, indifferent and disobedient living disqualify that person? Maybe it's true after all, it doesn't matter how you start, it only matters how you finish. So, maybe the path is much straighter and narrower than originally believed. Since faith without works is dead maybe there are a lot more people going to hell than we thought. Notwithstanding a so-called confession of faith, maybe living for the devil means that you will be dying with the devil as well.

If one concludes that this verse must cover all Christians (as is contended by most PTR apologists) then there are many fewer Christians than we think because that verse then means that Christians can *only* be those who watch and pray always. Yikes.

But indulge me for a moment. The ostensible purpose of the PTR teaching is to provide a measure of "comfort" regarding the Great Tribulation for Christians apparently fearful of having to endure tribulation. If this passage were in reference to skipping the Great Tribulation by a rapture, how does one know that he or she has watched enough and in fact, prayed "always" to a degree to know that they are counted worthy to escape? This artificial comfort level is most certainly denied Christians if this passage means what it implies --that removal by rapture is based upon a contingency of watching enough and praying always. But if the thought is that our very salvation itself is manifested or proven, in watching and praying always and not just a question of whether a Christian has done enough to make the cut to avoid the tribulation, then what is the assurance really being sought? The assurance we desire is that we won't be impacted by God's wrath, not that we won't be touched by Satan's tribulation. The assurance is of our salvation not our avoidance of a brief period of tribulation.

In Revelation Chapter 2, Jesus addresses the church at Ephesus and sets forth His issue with the church. He then says that to those who overcome, He will give them to eat from the tree of life. But doesn't that mean that if those church folks do not overcome that they don't get to eat of the tree of life? Jesus has issues with the church at Pergamos and then states that to those who overcome will He give some of the hidden manna to eat. Is not the converse that if they do not overcome then they do not get to eat of the hidden manna? Other promises for those who overcome are in other churches, again with converse applications, that is, that if they do not overcome then they will not enjoy the stated promise. Some of the promises sound like rewards in heaven but others sound more like heaven itself. Selah.

Now, consider the very last phrase of verse 36 that is never <u>ever</u> discussed. The reward for "watching and praying always" is stated right there in the verse and the reward is not being airlifted before the tribulation; it's to "stand before the Son of Man." Again, it means that if you don't watch and pray always, then you don't get to stand before the Son of Man. So, you can see that what you escape if you watch and pray always is God's wrath, not Satan's tribulation, as this seems to be a reference to salvation itself. To "stand before the Son of Man" has nothing to do with whether or not one makes a PTR but rather points directly to whether one will enjoy eternity with Jesus Christ. So enjoying eternity with Jesus Christ is inextricably linked to watching and praying always.

Now consider this. Even if the PTR were true, its advocates acknowledge that there are those who are saved after the PTR and so they too would certainly one day "stand before the Son of Man" as part of their reward. But how can that be their reward if that reward is inextricably linked to making the PTR as they interpret this passage? To "stand before the Son of Man" can only be linked to making it to heaven, not participating in a PTR.

To summarize, Christians go through the Great Tribulation. We are raptured at the end of the tribulation; however, we do not incur God's wrath. God's wrath and Satan's tribulation are two entirely different things. We have established that verse 36 regarding "watching and praying always" could apply just as appropriately to <u>an ability to endure</u> in the midst of tribulation as <u>removal</u> from tribulation. Those who are not watching and praying always are, at the least, candidates for Satan's wrath during the tribulation. Moreover, these "Christians" may be the sluggards referenced in verse 34 of Luke 21 or they might not be Christians at all.

Under any reasonable interpretation of this entire passage in Luke, nothing points to a PTR. Verse 36, by itself is equivocal but the entire passage is not. The only sure thing is that those who watch and pray always will not go through God's wrath. That's clear. Satan's tribulation is another story.

To repeat, equivocal evidence is no evidence at all. Though I cannot say that verse 36 by itself points to a post-tribulation rapture, it clearly does not prove a PTR rapture as supposed. Verse 36 calls into question the status of those who do not "watch and pray always." Indeed, if those who do not watch and pray always are not even Christians, then not making a supposed PTR is not their biggest problem. For those who watch and pray always however, the wrath of God does not even get close.

So here are your interpretational choices. (1) The passage refers to protection in the midst of the Great Tribulation. Christians will go through the

Great Tribulation but to those who watch and pray always, the "escape" will be their protection in the midst of the tribulation experience, not removal from it. Protection doesn't mean you won't be killed. It means that He will provide you the grace to bear up under the situation and the wrath of God does not come close. (2) The "yikes" alternative. The passage refers to escaping God's wrath, not the tribulation. Christians will go through the Great Tribulation but "Christian" means one who watches and prays always and who will escape God's wrath and stand before the Son of Man. Conversely, if you don't watch and pray always then you won't be protected in the midst of anything (tribulation or maybe God's wrath). Maybe you are not a Christian at all since failure to watch and pray may also mean that you won't stand before the Son of Man and that seems to imply that that you aren't even a Christian. But if my conclusion here is correct, the failure to watch and pray always, at the least, means that you won't enjoy a protection of grace in the depths of the tribulation.

As you may have noticed, the one interpretation not available is a PTR.

CHAPTER 8

THE STRAIGHT AND NARROW PATH
(AKA The Matthew 24 Nemesis)

It is said (and it is true) that the shortest distance between two points is a straight line. Unless we are taking the scenic route, we do not naturally take the long way to anywhere. Chapter 24 of the Book of Matthew is, without question, the single most comprehensive and straightforward chapter in the Bible dealing with the end times. While it is supplemented by the insight provided in Luke 21 which we just discussed, it is a direct, simple and chronological trip through to the last days' destination. In its plain and simple form, Matthew 24 is also a nemesis for PTR advocates and, as you will see, demands that the obvious be made confusing in order to make that suit fit.

This may be a good time to take a moment and re-read Matthew 24. The discourse gets underway in Verse 4 and in many ways tracks right along with the parallel passage that we just finished in Luke 21. Thus, some things will not be repeated but to reiterate, the "beginning of sorrows" (the beginning of the tribulation) will be marked by wars, famine and pestilence. However, one should note the first and foremost warning of Jesus relating to how we function in the last days. He says, "Take heed that no man deceive you." If there were not Christians on the earth at such a time, this comment would be meaningless. He surely would not be warning those currently lost in sin not to be deceived any more than they already are.

While the persecution of Christians was clear in Luke 21, it is even clearer in Matthew 24. Not only are we hated and reviled and many ultimately executed, it clearly states in verse 9 that we will be delivered up to *tribulation* then followed by execution. You read it correctly. We are delivered up to tribulation. Further, the beatings or torture only alluded to in Luke 21 are more apparent in Matthew 24. Since the tribulation ends with the death penalty, it is relatively safe to assume that lesser forms of brutality would precede the ultimate act. Again, we are reminded that *only* those who endure to the end shall be saved. So if you bail before then, it's hell for all eternity. Strong words, but the seriousness of the situation demands a serious warning.

Just how bad it becomes is clear from Verse 22 wherein Jesus states that if these days of tribulation were not shortened then no one would survive, but for the sake of the "elect" the Lord has actually shortened the time. This passage has demanded alteration by the PTR apologists lest the PTR theory self-destruct. To make everything fit, the "elect" can no longer be Christians; they must be Jews.

The terms "elect" and "election" appear far too many times in Scripture to embark upon a detailed analysis of the word but some explanation is required. To be "elect" or part of the "election" is to be "chosen." The terms have broad reach in the Word and it means, in various passages, those who have accepted Jesus Christ as Savior and, arguably, those who God, by His foreknowledge, knows will, in the process of time, come to Him. As such, "elect" and "election" can and do refer to Jewish believers, Gentile believers, the church and even Jesus Himself in several passages, but under no circumstances can one dogmatically conclude that the term only applies to believing Jews or Jews who will in time believe.

A good example comes from the parallel passage to Luke 21 and Matthew 24 found in Mark 13 wherein Jesus states, beginning in Verse 24 through Verse 27: (KJV):

> "But in those days <u>after</u> that <u>tribulation</u>, the sun shall be darkened, and the moon shall not give her light, and the stars of heaven shall fall, and the powers that are in heaven shall be shaken. And then shall they see the <u>Son of man coming</u>

<u>in the clouds</u> with great power and glory. And then shall he send his angels, and shall gather together his elect from the four winds, from the uttermost part of the <u>earth</u> to the uttermost part of <u>heaven</u>."

Angels gather together at one time, the saved from all across the earth to all across heaven. The rapture is occurring at a time <u>immediately</u> preceding His return or as part of His second coming (not a second coming before a third coming; once when He was born, once for a PTR and then a third coming at the end of the tribulation). So, who must the "elect" be? At the Lord's return He does not gather only Jews (be they believers or non-believers) from across the whole earth and then only Jewish believers from all across heaven. Certainly, those raptured are not only Jewish believers. The "elect" clearly are and only can be, in this most insightful passage, believers of all types and for all time.

The meaning of the word "elect" is simply altered to fit the PTR theory. The suit is tailored to fit a pre-ordained conclusion and once again that conclusion drives the interpretation of Scripture instead of allowing the plain meaning of Scripture to form the conclusion. But what we do have are a lot of Christians for whom the tribulation is severe and for whom God has simply shortened the time of endurance.

Verse 29 of Matthew 24 begins with the same passage cited above from Mark. Jesus states, "Immediately *after* the tribulation of those days..." What tribulation is Jesus referring to? The tribulation He just finished describing as being so bad it needed to be cut short. *Then* the signs and wonders in the sky would occur and *then* He returns. As noted in the parallel passage from Mark, then and *only* then does He collect His saints from around the world (i.e., the rapture) *and* from heaven in which the dead in Christ rise before those who are alive and remain (I Thessalonians 4) and are caught up with those who were raised from the dead. The virtual simultaneous events of the collection of saints who are living (rapture) along with the gathering of saints who have died (raised from the dead and the spirits of whom are collected from across heaven) is nothing short of beautiful in its simplicity. The order of events is clear and straightforward and the fact that Christians are on the earth, preparing to be raptured after the tribulation, is so transparent from the text, that it requires biblical gymnastics to alter the obvious.

I have said that there is no single passage that proves the PTR, but if there is one (and there are a couple actually) that single-handedly proves the PTR to be incorrect, it would be this passage from Mark. The virtual simultaneous collection of saints from heaven and earth (rapture-though we know the ones from heaven at least momentarily precede the ones on earth) relayed in this passage is so clearly stated to follow the tribulation and the sun and moon darkening along with other tribulation events that the PTR theory is utterly untenable. That is unless you can somehow place the sun and moon darkening and all the other tribulation events referenced in this passage as actually occurring before the tribulation! The PTR theory here requires that the events of the tribulation precede the rapture that precedes the tribulation. This is what I meant earlier when I stated that it's difficult to un-convolute a convoluted theory without getting a headache.

While II Thessalonians 2 will be discussed separately, it should be noted that this, more or less, simultaneous collection of saints (living and deceased) immediately prior to or part of Jesus' second coming, is also referenced in II Thessalonians 2. The first verse of this chapter begins with "Now brethren, concerning the coming of our Lord Jesus Christ _and_ our gathering together unto Him...." These two events, His coming (return) _and_ our gathering together (collection of the saints both on earth and heaven) are occurring virtually simultaneously. The coming is the second coming, not as PTR apologists imply from I Thessalonians 4, that being an intermediate return just sufficient to greet the saints in the clouds, hit the brakes, do a u-turn and beat it back to heaven. PTR apologists would lead you to believe that He comes just enough to grab the saints but does not descend quite far enough for it to be called the second coming. Further, the context of this passage is clear in its reference to a post-tribulation rapture since several verses later, this "gathering together" does not occur until *after* the unveiling of the anti-Christ. Obviously you cannot be raptured before the anti-Christ's "coming out" when the passage itself states that it can't happen until after his unveiling.

Furthermore, consider Revelation 1:7 which states:

> "Behold he (Jesus) cometh with clouds (rapture); and every eye shall see him, and they also which pierced him: and all kindred's of the earth shall wail, because of him. Even so, Amen."

This verse referencing the virtually combined event of His second coming and the rapture, how would the whole earth see Him and mourn if, as the PTR advocates contend, He only comes half-way, vanishing out of sight and then returns to heaven? Yes we're whisked away in the twinkling of an eye, but that doesn't mean that no one sees what else is happening, that being, Jesus' return. They do see, they do mourn and wail. So you can see that the whole thing about planes crashing and cars going off the road and everyone left on earth wondering what happened at the time of the rapture for years afterward (and everything else associated with the *Left Behind* series) is raw fiction.

Indeed, if Jesus is not actually returning in a complete sense at the time of the rapture, a good question is why any meeting in the clouds is necessary at all. Why are not the saints who are raptured simply raptured all the way to heaven? People who subscribe to the PTR always make reference to the Lord returning any day now, that "He could return at any moment," when they really do not mean what they are saying. As a PTR supporter they are really saying, "At any moment, He could come half-way." Of course, in the great majority of these people, it is said in good faith and belief, but it is not correct.

The terms, "Day of the Lord," the "coming of the Lord" and "second coming" are all one and the same. When Jesus returns to set up His kingdom, it is referred to as His "second coming." But the use of that term suggests why a PTR return must be called something else in order to avoid the PTR becoming the second coming since His return to establish His kingdom at the end of the tribulation, of necessity, would then become His third coming.

Again, the "coming of the Son of man" is referenced in Verse 37 of Matthew 24, entirely in the context of the reference to Noah (the deliverance of which PTR apologists universally contend to be a "type" of the rapture), yet the PTR apologists refuse to allow for the verses that follow to describe the rapture. The reason? If Verses 40 and 41 of Matthew 24 relate to the rapture, then for yet another reason the PTR theory implodes. Those verses state:

> "Then shall two be in the field; the one shall be taken and the other left. Two women shall be

grinding at the mill; the one shall be taken and the other left."

If this is the rapture, the text places it at the end/after the tribulation. Neither the hour nor day of His return is known.

The standard PTR response to the Matthew 24: 40-41 dilemma is to contend that the person taken is taken in judgment and the person left is simply an unsaved person who will remain until Jesus returns to set up the millennial kingdom (since he didn't take the mark of the beast so as to be taken also). This was the position of a PTR advocate with whom I engaged in a recent semi-debate on radio. The problem is that neither the text nor the context of the passage allows for such a conclusion. The passage continues in its reference to how people were swept away at the time of the flood because they weren't ready. This is further underscored at the end of the passage by Jesus' reference to Himself coming as a thief in the night and catching people unprepared. The emphasis is clearly upon the need to watch and be prepared for His return since the exact time would not be known.

The PTR advocates contend that neither of these two (the one taken and the one left behind) are believers since believers all left in the PTR. So the obvious question arises, "Why would the ones swept away to judgment be watching for His return and why would the ones remaining be looking for Jesus' return since they aren't believers?" Jesus' admonitions to watch is wasted breathe, if neither of these two people is Christian. The only explanation that makes sense of this passage is that the one taken is Christian and is taken in a post-tribulation rapture just before Jesus' return and the other is left to deal with the fallout of not being saved at His return. If he were saved, he'd be taken too. But this is yet another example of the conclusion-driven nature of the PTR theory. The conclusion is simply that the PTR is a fact. There-fore, this passage must mean something other than the obvious.

It should be noted that a minority of PTR advocates, in acknowledging the highly-strained interpretation given to this passage to hold the PTR position together, contend that if this passage does refer to the rapture of the one taken, then this passage is chronologically out of order. However, this minority position still proves my point. All available, if not strained, interpretations and renderings need to be considered if what is at stake is the PTR theory itself.

As I mentioned in the beginning of this book, the Word is a covenant, a contract if you will. As an attorney, attention is given to words for which, if there is no obvious reason to conclude that the words are symbolic or metaphorical, a literal meaning should be applied. After all, the Holy Spirit is not a sloppy writer. He means what He says and wouldn't be casual in assumptions and approximations. Thus, when He says that no man knows the day or the hour, He means "day" or "hour." Beyond that though, are weeks and months. Could we know the week or the month? Certainly, since it was not excluded and Scripture firmly proves that a knowing or approximation of that time will be experienced by watchful saints. Thus, the Lord's return and our catching away should not catch Christians by surprise (Matthew 24:44, I Thessalonians 5:4 and numerous other passages).

Of course, many contend that Jesus' use of the terms "day" and "hour" is metaphorical and should not be taken literally. However, the only reason to not take their usage literally is that it weakens the PTR theory. By no means do I suggest by the following comment that PTR apologists are evolutionists but the Lord's use of the term "day" in the creation account is a use to which we readily (and correctly, I should add) admit to being a literal day, not a metaphorical day. Why the change in meaning here? The answer is that if more than the day or hour is "knowable" then there is no imminent return or surprise catching away of the saints, two concurrent themes running through PTR advocacy. It means that there are events that will precede His return that will provide significant insight that those who are watching will recognize. There are clues, but these more precise and specific clues are largely given inside the tribulation experience itself. Since the more precise clues occur in and during the tribulation itself, a PTR, of necessity must be proffered as an event without warning since the key warnings don't occur before the tribulation starts. In other words, if you are raptured before the more precise clues are given, then yes, you will be clueless and hence a surprise rapture. However, because the Lord does give precise clues here, maybe even narrowing down to the week or month, there won't be the total surprise that the PTR theory demands. These clues for those watching and praying always will keep the watchful informed and as such, there will be no great surprise in the timing of the rapture.

In Revelation 9:15, the Lord is very precise in His use and distinction between the words, "hour," "day," "month" and "year." That same standard should be applied throughout Scripture except where the meta-phorical use is obvious.

I Thessalonians 5 describes Jesus' return as a thief in the night for which we should be prepared and watching, or as with the 10 virgins described in Matthew, prepared for His return. Many quote I Thessalonians 5:2, that the "day of the Lord so cometh as a thief in the night" to make the same point that we, since we know neither the day nor hour of His return, have no way to anticipate and prepare for any certain event. What is omitted frequently in that recitation are the next two verses from I Thessalonians 5:3-4 (KJV), which state:

> "For when they shall say, Peace and safety; then sudden destruction cometh upon them, as

travail upon a woman with child; and they shall not escape. <u>But</u> ye, brethren, are <u>not</u> in darkness, that that day should overtake you as a thief."

Translated, Jesus has no intention of leaving His own in the dark. Not only is it obvious from this passage that Christians are here on earth at the time of the PTR but also to the present point, they will not be caught off guard. They will not be without warning or notice. It will not be the surprise catching away that PTR apologists' state. To get us out of here before the tribulation occurs requires that we have no real idea of the timing of His return, something that Scripture actually does not support. Indeed, the very existence of the signs, warnings and notices, which are embedded within the tribulation period itself strip the PTR theory of the ignorance required of His return in order to support that theory.

In other words, Christians may not know the day or hour, but they can get pretty close. They just won't know until the time gets close just how close they are. Does not Jesus admonish the Jews for not seeing the signs of the times in Matthew though they knew how to read the sky that portended bad weather? These more general signs were expected by Jesus to be known even by those without having the benefit of the presence of the Holy Spirit. How much more so would those who have the Holy Spirit in them have a more precise sense of His return? Knowing the signs is half of the equation. The other half is watching.

Let's make it simpler. If the tribulation period contains the signs of Jesus' return then you would have to be in the tribulation to observe those signs. If we were raptured before the tribulation we wouldn't be here to observe them. But since the Word makes it clear that the brethren will know these things and will not be left in darkness, the saints then must be in the tribulation to gain that knowledge of the true immanency of His return.

In summary, Matthew 24, as supplemented by Mark 13, shows that Christians will be around for the tribulation. They may or may not survive the tribulation. If they do, they will be raptured at the end of the tribulation right after the saints who have passed away rise from the dead and then just before or part of Jesus' second coming. That rapture is not the surprise that it is described to be by PTR apologists. Those who are watching and praying will be ready and prepared as their "redemption draweth nigh." They will look up because they will know the approximate time, just not the precise time. The brethren who are watching are not in darkness. Therefore, that day shall not catch them by surprise as a thief in the night would catch those who are not watching.

CHAPTER 9

COULD THE LORD REALLY RETURN ANY DAY ?

"The Lord could return at any time." I have heard that my entire Christian life and did not doubt it for years. In fact, earlier in life it would have been borderline heresy to question the truth of that statement. Yet, as I have studied Scripture over the last forty years, my view has changed. There indeed *will come a day* when He could return at any moment since, at that point in time, we will not know the hour or the day. But that return is His return at the end of the age. That will be His *only* return. This chapter will bring forth yet another piece of evidence from Scripture that points this out. Not only does II Thessalonians 2:1-4 provide yet more scriptural evidence of the fact that the rapture occurs at the end of the tribulation as set forth in the previous chapter, it also makes clear that the rapture absolutely will not occur until certain events have come to pass and thus cannot happen at any moment.

The passage is as follows:

"(1) Now brethren, concerning the coming of our Lord Jesus Christ and our gathering together to Him, we ask you, (2) not to be soon shaken in mind or troubled, either by spirit or by word or by letter as if from us, as though the day of Christ had come. (3) Let no one deceive you by any means for *that Day will not come* unless the falling away comes first, and the man of sin is revealed, the son of perdition, (4) who opposes and exalts himself above all that is called God or that is worshiped, so that he sits as God in the temple of God, showing himself that he is God,"

The key verses are 1 and 3. Note that two events occur in verse 1, the coming of the Lord and our gathering together to Him. The conjunction "and" makes it clear that the two events are connected. They are related and the text implies that they occur at virtually the same time. To interpret them as separate and un-related would be as if I said, "Before the leaves turn this fall <u>and</u> before I wash my car, I need to fertilize the lawn." You cannot conjoin two events that have nothing to do with each other and make sense. But consider if I said, "Before the leaves turn this fall <u>and</u> before I have to rake them up, I need to get the lawn fertilized." The leaves turning and raking the leaves that subsequently fall are intimately connected, occur-ring at almost the same time as one event leads directly to the other.

The word "and" conjoins two separate but intimately related events in this verse that are so connected as to occur essentially at the same time with one precipitating the other. Our "gathering together to Him" can only mean the rapture and it isn't separable from His coming. We are not all gathered together at any other time and it occurs and is connected with the coming of the Lord. As has been established earlier, the Lord Jesus Christ does not return at the time of a PTR (constituting the second return out of what would then have to be three comings). Instead, consistent with all other references in Scripture, He returns at the very end of the age when He comes to judge the earth and set up His kingdom. There is no evidence for the PTR proposition that the "coming of the Lord Jesus Christ" refers to a descent half-way to earth where He meets the saints and concludes the trip with a u-turn in the sky. However, that is the definition of "coming" that is required, lest the PTR theory comes to an end. There is one other explanation but I will address that in a moment.

So the Lord returns at the end of the age and His coming is directly and intimately associated <u>with</u> our gathering together to Him (i.e., the rapture). But this is hardly where the discussion ends since additional evidence will now be introduced to show that our gathering together can *only* mean a post-tribulation rapture and not a PTR. Verse 3 states, "Let no man deceive you by any means; for that day *will not come....*"What "day" are we talking about? It's an obvious reference to verse 1, the day of the "coming of our Lord Jesus Christ <u>and</u> our gathering together to Him."

In other words, the verse opens up the fact that "that day", the coming of our Lord and the rapture cannot occur until certain other, well-identified events occur. The first event that must occur is a great falling away, described in the Greek as "apostasia," from which we get our word "apostasy." So the coming of our Lord Jesus Christ and the rapture cannot occur until apostasy occurs, which by compelling implication, is not a localized event. Apostasy is a strong word and it reveals not just a general moral decline occurring over an extended period of time but rather a more decided and purposeful rejection and refutation of the Gospel. Indeed, the point should be argued that the falling away or apostasy does not reveal a condition of society as much as it reveals a condition of the church. To make this passage accommodate a PTR though, PTR advocates must dilute the meaning of this word, making apostasy to be a general decline and departure from God's word throughout society. But apostasy has no application to the general public without depriving the word of its very meaning. After all, how does someone who does not know the Lord fall away? They are not close to Him to begin with. Must you not first be near before you can then fall away? It isn't apostasy for a non-believer to become even more "non-believing" or for a heathen to become a greater heathen. The question that is begged is, are Christians the ones falling away since apostasy is an impossibility for pagans.

Suffice it to say that one of the precursors to the rapture is a worldwide or at least a very widespread turning away from the Gospel by people who, at a minimum, used to occupy pews. Their hearts have turned cold as it states in Matthew 24, which again, must mean that they were once warm or passionate for the souls of mankind. These people, if not fallen souls who once embraced the Gospel, now have become spectators, non-participants or possibly the new persecutors of the ones with whom they used to identify. If some Christians start to waffle in their stand for the Lord as the tribulation deepens, that would really be no surprise.

But the PTR theory requires that the church be raptured followed by an immediate move of the Holy Spirit (to produce all new saints on the earth during the tribulation who missed the rapture because they weren't saved in time). But then all the new converts immediately start to fall away? Apostasy is far more likely to occur among those who never experienced persecution such as the lukewarm church of Laodicea that goes into tribulation. It seems impossible to occur in the lives of those individuals who, while in the tribulation, see the error of their ways, accept the Lord but then immediately start to fall away.

This "falling away" passage raises two questions. First, could a widespread apostasy occur before the beginning of the tribulation thereby accommodating a PTR theory? Second, what would cause this widespread apostasy?

The answer is yes to the first question. If this were the only consideration in the interpretation of this passage, there could be widespread apostasy that occurs *prior* to a PTR. But that is not all there is to the verse. Once again, we have one of those pesky conjunctions restricting our interpretation options. The verse says that not only must there be this great falling away prior to the rapture but that *also*, the "man of sin, the son of perdition" must be revealed. No one argues with the fact that the personality referenced is none other than the anti-Christ. What is again conjoined, or intimately connected, is the apostasy occurring at or approximately during the time of the revelation of the anti-Christ.

Now, whether or not you agree with the assertions just set forth relating to what can or will constitute apostasy, however "apostasy" is defined, or what it means in this context, that is not the real problem that PTR apologists face in this passage. The crux of the PTR problem lies with the second requirement before our "gathering together" (i.e. rapture) can occur. Whether from the Book of Daniel, Matthew 24 or other passages, it is a universally accepted fact that the revelation of the anti-Christ occurs three and one-half years prior to the return of the Lord. This event is described elsewhere as the "abomination of desolation" and II Thessalonians 2:4 capsulizes this event. So if the rapture (the gathering together of the saints from Verse 1) happens at the same time as His coming and these two events can't occur until the abomination of desolation occurs three and one-half years into the tribulation, then how could the rapture precede the beginning of this seven year period? In other words, the rapture can't precede by three and one-half years the very event, namely the abomination of desolation which we have just read must come before the rapture. The only logical interpretation of this passage is that half-way through the tribulation the anti-Christ is revealed *after* which Jesus returns with his just-raptured saints. Put yet another way, how can what could only happen on Wednesday precede that which could only happen two days earlier on Monday? Wednesday follows Monday just as the rapture follows after the abomination of desolation that occurs halfway through the tribulation. This is a devastating default in logic in the PTR doctrine.

The only real argument by PTR apologists can be that the "gathering together" is not the rapture. This would be a tortured interpretation. The words are so plain and forthright. When would our "gathering together with Him" occur if not when all the saints on earth and resurrected saints (Mark 13:27) are gathered together at the time of the rapture? We aren't gathered together at any other time.

But this comment leads to another comment that must be stated. As I have said before (and will reference again), PTR doctrine really starts with a conclusion and works backwards to find its justification in Scripture. To make the point, if a PTR apologist stated that "our gathering together unto Him" is not a reference to a post-tribulation rapture, upon what authority could that be based? None. It would be based upon the raw assumption that it simply can't be so because there's no post-tribulation rapture. Why not? Because the rapture occurs before the tribulation. You see, the assumption drives the interpretation of Scripture instead of the Scriptures producing the interpretation.

Suppose for a moment that you could erase all teaching regarding end times and that you read our passage under consideration for the first time. Is there any conceivable way you could emerge from the reading with a PTR conclusion? No. While I mentioned that you have to be taught a PTR perspective, this little exercise proves why. It's because the plain reading and chronological assessment of Scripture will dictate a conclusion different than a PTR conclusion unless you've been taught otherwise.

You may think that with our first question resolved the answer to the other question (what would cause the widespread apostasy) has now been rendered moot.

Nothing more needs to be proven here to further disprove a PTR. However, the fact that great apostasy accompanies the unveiling of the anti-Christ is clearly set forth and should be addressed. It seems rather understandable with the revealing of a world dictator, who, with great power and intimidation, demands to be worshiped, that there would then be a great falling away due to raw fear. I have seen in our church how little it takes for some people to cut and run when taking a stand for traditional (biblical) marriage as such a stand would cause them to risk being in the crosshairs of the homosexual community. That is kindergarten stuff compared to life under the rule of the anti-Christ. Why would we be surprised that some people fall away when the evil and persecution of the anti-Christ is fully manifested against the saints? In fact, it would be perplexing if such a falling away among some did not occur if they thought that by falling away, as in compromising with the anti-Christ, they might save their lives.

It is a bit of a digression from the focus of this chapter, but it seems to be the best time to discuss a verse that comes only a few verses after the passage under discussion. While we are in the neighborhood, I will conclude with an analysis of the supposed PTR evidence set forth in II Thessalonians 2:7 which states: "For the mystery of lawlessness is already at work; only He who now restrains will do so until He is taken out of the way." The "He" in this passage is alternately considered by PTR apologists to be either the church or the Holy Spirit but frequently it is concluded to be the church (i.e., evidence of the rapture).

If this did refer to the church, the passage suggests that the "He" being removed is what allows for the revelation of the anti-Christ. Since the revelation of the anti-Christ is in the middle of the tribulation, not the beginning, there is a problem because the PTR theory requires that the rapture be before the beginning of the tribulation. If the church is the restrainer, then that restraint would operate right up to the point in time of the anti-Christ's unveiling. In no way can the "He" be the church. If the church is removed before the tribulation begins and the church is the restrainer, then what restrains the anti-Christ for three and one-half years of the tribulation leading up to the time of his coming out?

The "He" is not the church nor is it the Holy Spirit. Throughout the Book of Revelation it is obvious that there are many Christians on earth during the tribulation. In Revelation, Chapter 7, the implication is that it could be in the hundreds of thousands if not millions of Christians that are on the earth during the tribulation since Revelation 7:9 makes reference to a "great multitude which no one could number of all nations, tribes, peoples and tongues" who are clearly identified in Revelation 7:14 as ones who came out of the Great Tribulation. They were not removed prior to the Great Tribulation; they came out of it which could be by death during the tribulation or rapture at the end. But it is not before the tribulation. You can't "come out" of something before that something has even begun. Many faithful are killed during the reign of the anti-Christ as this is clear from Revelation 20:4 (and other verses) that reference those who will be beheaded for not taking the mark of the beast.

The mark of the beast does not exist prior to the tribulation nor likely before the anti-Christ's full emergence which is halfway through the tribulation. While persecution likely increases through the first three and one-half years, the Christian holocaust really begins halfway through the tribulation. This is because at the revelation of the anti-Christ's identity half-way through the tribulation, the limitations of persecution against Christians owing to a concealed identity are now removed. But the key issue is that since there are unmistakably untold thousands of Christians on earth during some part of the tribulation, has the church been removed? Of course not. Jesus said that where two or more are gathered in His name, that He would be in the midst of them. Sounds like church to me.

Some note that the word "church," which is used frequently in the first several chapters of Revelation is not mentioned after the third chapter and that this is a sign of the departure of the church (i.e., the PTR). There is a saying in law that if you have three arguments to make, one excellent, one good and one fair, that you get rid of the good and fair. If it is fair, then it has a lot of holes; if it is good, it does not have many holes but it still has some. If it is excellent, it is bulletproof and that is what you want. In this case, this argument is less than fair. It's hollow. To focus on the mere presence of the word "church" as the litmus test for whether a "church" exists thereafter lacks all interpretational logic. Not only do subsequent chapters reveal two or more believers gathered together but in fact multitudes of Christians exist on the earth. For that matter, one could look at all the books in the New Testament and find that the word "church" is frequently absent. Would one conclude that because the actual word "church" is not used in all these other books that no church was in fact present?

Next, since no one comes to the Lord but by the Holy Spirit, it cannot be the Holy Spirit that has been removed. How do all these thousands/millions of Christians on earth for some part of the tribulation function but for the presence of the Holy Spirit working in and among them? Whether they are Christians who have been around for a while (because there was no PTR) or Christians who just became Christians during the tribulation (which is the PTR explanation for their presence), the Holy Spirit can't be absent if believers are present.

So who is the "He" in this verse? Whoever or whatever the "He" represents He is only taken out of the way. It does not say that "He" has been removed. So it could be the Holy Spirit but not in the way PTR apologists proffer. The Holy Spirit simply is no longer the restraint for a period of time and for this specific and limited purpose. All the praying by the saints at that time will not invoke the power of the Holy Spirit for the purpose of stopping the anti-Christ. But again this is a specific and limited non-engagement. It is not the by -product of total absence or removal of the Holy Spirit but rather a period of standing down.

Furthermore, and I cannot be dogmatic about this, it may be a reference to one of the archangels, Michael or Gabriel. In Daniel Chapter 10, the angel Michael is the breakthrough in a battle with a demonic adversary ruling politically over Persia. So not only do we know that angels are involved in battles over earthly kingdoms, but the role of the Holy Spirit in standing down would likely be implemented through that/those angel(s) who have been actively engaged against the anti-Christ until the order to stand down is given. They do not leave or go on sabbatical for a couple of years; they simply give space for this event only so as to allow for the unmasking of the anti-Christ to fulfill his calling.

From here, we will turn our attention to a mystery rarely discussed.

CHAPTER 10

THE LAST TRUMPET

My mother played both trumpet and piano and insisting I pick up an instrument; she let me use her trumpet in my early school years, that is, until I put a dent in it. After that, she did not want me to play that instrument anymore and seemed surprisingly accommodating of having me pick up the guitar instead (though she was probably hoping that I actually would damage that). However, I have always loved the sound of the trumpet. From *Taps* to *Reveille,* to the beginning of the Kentucky Derby; from Winton Marsalis to Franz Von Suppe and his *Light Cavalry Overture* (which causes me to want to mount an unknown horse, ride off to an unknown battle, all for an unknown cause), the trumpet does it all. It wakes soldiers in the morning and sends them to bed at night. Its clarion call is used for battle, for Mexican weddings and for New Orleans funerals, but more importantly, it will be used to raise the dead at the time of the rapture. It will be one exciting day beyond all description and expectation. I understand that the word trumpet likely means the shofar, though different in sound, possesses some of the same essential qualities. So it comes as no surprise to me that the Lord would use the sound of a trumpet to herald that day. In the quintessential rapture passage in I Thessalonians 4:16-17 it states as follows:

> "For the Lord Himself will descend from heaven with a shout, with the voice of an archangel, and with the trumpet of God. And the dead in Christ will rise first. Then we who are alive and remain shall be caught up together with them in the clouds to meet the Lord in the air. And thus we shall always be with the Lord."

This is not the only passage however, referencing the trumpet at the second coming of our Lord. In I Corinthians15:51-52 (NKJV), it states:

> "Behold I tell you a mystery. We shall not all sleep, but we shall all be changed in a moment, in the twinkling of an eye, at the last trumpet. For the trumpet will sound, and the dead will be raised incorruptible, and we shall be changed."

Note that now the description of His return is a bit more specific. It is not just a trumpet; it is the last trumpet. The passage may well be a key clue to the timing of the Lord's return.

The word "last" obviously means that there is more than one trumpet involved. Obviously there would be no way of knowing what trumpet is the last trumpet unless you also knew just how many trumpets there are altogether. The use of the phrase "last trumpet" is a sign relating to the timing of this event of the ages. It must be a clue or sign to us because God certainly does not need a reminder or sticky note of when He is supposed to blow the trumpet. His word is for us.

So what is the significance of the last trumpet? In Revelation, Chapter 8, the Lord begins a series of judgments on the earth, each heralded by an angel that blows a trumpet to initiate that judgment. While the judgments are severe, they are not universal. While the judgments are visited upon the earth, not everyone on earth is visited by the judgments. In each situation, the impact is felt by only a portion of the earth, such as one-third of the streams, one-third of the living creatures in the sea, one-third of the ships in the ocean, etc. Thus, it is significant that two-thirds of these elements are not touched and, as I mentioned in a previous chapter, may reflect the fact that there are those on the earth upon whom these judgments are not to fall.

I'm not suggesting that Christians are around during and through all of God's judgments. But they could be here during some and be miraculously protected as God protected the Jews from the Egyptian plagues beginning with the fourth plague. What is clear though, is that Christians are here during the tribulation, the outpouring of Satan's wrath. Satan has no reason to take his wrath out on unbelievers. Unbelievers are not his nemesis - Israel and Christians are. Chapter 12 of Revelation also makes it clear that both Jews and Christians are his target as it references in Revelation 12:17 that not only is Satan enraged at Israel, but also "her offspring" who bear the testimony of Jesus Christ. If you love Jesus, this is talking about you.

There are seven trumpets in all and, as in the passage from I Thessalonians 4:16 an angel sounds the trumpet. The trumpet which is used for the rapture (the last trumpet) is blown by a high-ranking angel, an archangel. So, putting these two verses together which speak to the same event, it is clear that it is an archangel who blows the last trumpet that is the call for the resurrection of the dead. So could the "last" trumpet referenced in I Corinthians 15 be the last, or seventh trumpet, which is described in Revelation 11:15-19? We have no other multiple trumpets sounding anywhere else during the tribulation or anywhere else in Scripture for that matter from which a determination of the "last" trumpet could even be considered. The answer is "yes."

If the first six trumpets announce a judgment upon the earth, it might not seem appropriate that a seventh trumpet announcing a resurrection of the just from the dead would be associated with a seventh judgment. But this is where the trumpet chronology makes a chilling turn. It is not initially a time of judgment at all. Consider the passage beginning in Revelation 11:15 (NKJV):

> "Then the seventh angel sounded: And there were loud voices in heaven, saying "The kingdoms of this world have become the kingdoms of our Lord and of His Christ, and He shall reign forever and ever!" And the twenty-four elders who sat before God on their thrones fell on their faces and worshiped God."

While this may be setting the stage for the Lord's return and judgment upon the earth, this trumpet by itself does not launch that event.

While much judgment is yet to ensue, this passage is not about judgment *per se*. It is a time of celebration and would not this be the fitting time for the dead in Christ to be raised? Would not the resurrection of the dead in Christ be part of the celebration? For six angels and six trumpets, we have had judgments, but at the sound of the seventh trumpet, the last trumpet, there is a celebration instead, a celebration so magnificent that it inspired Handel's *Messiah*. And would it not be fitting that it is an archangel that blows this trumpet? The last trumpet is a sound of victory, of resurrection from the dead. This is no coincidence. God seems to be giving us a clue when in the course of the tribulation the rapture would occur. The last trumpet is the trumpet of resurrection and <u>no</u> other Scripture fits this event. No other trumpet fits this event.

The final passage dealing with the last trumpet is the rapture passage, previously cited from Matthew 24:29-31(KJV), which states:

> "Immediately <u>after the tribulation </u>of those days shall the sun be darkened, and the moon shall not give her light, and the stars shall fall from heaven, and the powers of the heavens shall be shaken: And then shall appear the sign of the Son of man in heaven: and then shall all the tribes of the earth mourn, and they shall see the Son of man coming in the clouds of heaven with power and great glory. And he shall send his angels <u>with a great sound of a trumpet</u>, and they shall gather together his elect from the four winds, from one end of heaven to the other."

The order of events could not be clearer. The passage starts with a period beginning <u>after</u> the tribulation; <u>then</u> we have cataclysmic events in the sky and the Lord returns with the whole world seeing His return. The last trumpet blows and <u>then</u> and only then does He rapture His church. It is further underscored by the parallel passage in Mark which states that what is gathered together is not only from one end of heaven to the other, it is also from one end of the earth to the other.

The whole earth sees this event and mourns. So would this be the supposed u-turn in the sky as PTR apologists contend occurs in I Thessalonians 4? Or does this occur after the tribulation when, subsequent to the meeting in the sky with the Lord, the descent is completed so that the whole earth can see it? Seeing this event and mourning does not seem the likely response to a halfway visitation in the clouds and immediate departure from there back out of sight. The word does not make clear how much time elapses in the sky or what else transpires on earth during this time and I will not speculate since, for those who have been raised from the dead and for those just raptured, time has become a meaningless concept.

There is one thing the Word does not support though and that is a return to heaven. The return to heaven is simply what "must happen" if the PTR theory is to make sense. However it is difficult to imagine the starting of an event that is not finished. And where is the coming with "great power and glory" if His descent is no closer than in the clouds followed by a retreat to heaven? And it is a trumpet-blowing archangel who announces a great and glorious return, not half of a return.

Before we finish this discussion about the role of the trumpet section in God's orchestra, a further but serious flaw of the PTR theory should be noted in this context. According to PTR doctrine, before the start of the tribulation, the church is raptured. But since the church is raptured <u>after</u> the blowing of the <u>last</u> trumpet how can the last trumpet blow before anything has even begun? In other words, if nothing has yet begun at the sound of the last trumpet, then for what purpose did all the previous trumpets sound before the last one? If nothing has begun because we're still in pre-tribulation mode here, then what would those trumpets be announcing? The answer is "nothing." The trumpet-blowing events all occur after the tribulation begins. That is abundantly clear. So if all the trumpet-blowing events occur during the tribulation, how then can the last trumpet be blown before the tribulation even starts? The PTR theory forces you to believe that the last trumpet somehow precedes all the trumpets that come before it. It can't but these are the kinds of time-line brainteasers that the PTR theory forces us to unpack when exposing the flaws in the theory.

The answer lies in the fact that all the trumpets are being blown, as we have seen, during and well into the tribulation. Clearly the last trumpet cannot be blown prior to the trumpets before it and the last trumpet cannot be blown prior to the occurrence of the events that the earlier trumpets announce.

Armageddon is not the event that the seventh angel and the seventh (last) trumpet proclaims. Instead, the seventh trumpet is a "break in the action" as some might say but it is radically different than the first six trumpet judgments. I cannot be dogmatic about this but something very different is in play at this point in the judgment and trumpet chronology. Could it be that this is when we finally get out of here? It appears so.

CHAPTER 11

WORKING OVERTIME TO
AVOID BEING HONORED

Why do so many PTR advocates and apologists work so hard to avoid being honored? You are likely wondering what I am talking about, but the fact is that the Christians who survive the tribulation or are martyred in the course of it, are "highly decorated veterans," if you will. The Bible reveals numerous passages detailing not only the price that they pay, but also the honor and reward they receive for enduring to the end. No one else receives the recognition that the tribulation saints are awarded.

First, it should be noted that this has always been God's plan. Those that have been persecuted for their faith have always received special honor and reward. Our spiritual forerunners from the 11th Chapter of Hebrews, also known as the Faith Hall of Fame, are an example. In fact, saints who suffer persecution (past, present and future) are noted for special recognition as Jesus points out in His Sermon on the Mount wherein

He states in Matthew 5: 10-12 (NKJV):

> "Blessed are those who are <u>persecuted</u> for right-eousness sake, for theirs is the kingdom of heaven. Blessed are you when they revile you and persecute you, and say all kinds of evil against you falsely for My sake. Rejoice and be exceedingly glad for great is your <u>reward</u> in heaven, for so they persecuted the prophets who were before you."

The faith-filled exploits of those who have gone before us are noteworthy indeed but none are awarded the degree of recognition provided the end-time martyrs in the Book of Revelation.

Some of these passages have been addressed in other contexts but they should be noted here beginning with Revelation 2:10 (NKJV), which states:

> "Do not fear any of those things which you are about to suffer. Indeed, the devil is about to throw some of you into prison, that you may be tested and will have tribulation ten days. Be faithful until death, and I will give you the crown of life."

So we have saints in the tribulation who are impris-oned and then pay the ultimate price with their life but the Word states that those who endure under these trying circumstances are rewarded with a crown of life.

It is significant that the phrase "crown of life" is earned by means of paying the ultimate price in a time of tribulation. Interestingly, the only other time this phrase is used in the entire Bible is in James 1:12 (NKJV), where it states:

> "Blessed is the man who endures temptation (testing), for when he has been approved, he shall receive the crown of life which the Lord has promised to those who love Him."

Note that in each of the only two passages where this phrase is used, the crown of life is obtained by passing tests and trials which most of us would prefer to avoid. It is not a prerequisite to going to heaven, as there are those who have never been and will never be severely tested. However, the fact is that those who obtain the crown of life by enduring and passing through tribulation are the ones who receive this special recognition in Scripture. Yes, all who love Him get the crown but those who came by it the hard way get written about in God's Word. It is more than just an "honorable mention." While it may be speculation, who knows whether those other honors and rewards are bestowed specially upon those who had/have to prove their love the hardest way of all - with their life.

So the question is this: Would it be *eternally* more beneficial to go to heaven without having to go through tribulation or is it *eternally* more beneficial to go to heaven having successfully endured trials and sufferings without renouncing our Lord even unto death? If successfully enduring trials and tribulations were eternally of greater reward, then why would we follow a theological doctrine whereby that opportunity is eliminated? Why would we adhere to a doctrine that would deprive us this honor?

In Revelation 6:9-11(NKJV), it states in reference to the cry of the martyrs upon the opening of the 5th seal:

> "When He opened the fifth seal, I saw under the altar the souls of those who had been slain for the word of God and for the testimony which they held. And they cried with a loud voice saying "How long, O Lord, holy and true, until You judge and avenge our blood on those who dwell on the earth?" Then a white robe was given to each of them; and it was said to them that they should rest a little while longer, until both the number of their fellow servants and their brethren, who would be killed as they were, was completed."

First, note that these are all tribulation saints. So the context is during the tribulation wherein there are a lot of Christians who are being slaughtered for the Gospel.

Again, as with the prior passage, those who endure this ordeal successfully receive a reward—here a white robe. It is clear elsewhere that there are robes of righteousness received by Christians who may not have suffered in the manner or to the extent that these Christians suffer but here the robe is handed out in direct response to their successful endurance to the end. As with the saints in Revelation 2:10, these saints also have paid the ultimate price - their life. Adding to the price they have paid is the obvious anguish expressed in what seems like a delay in justice. Apparently, the administration of justice is yet premature and presumably because the offense is not yet complete (i.e., more saints have to be executed); there is some waiting to do. Likely, this group grows as the executed saints keep coming to take their place under the altar so to speak and yes, it would seem that those also would get their robes at such time.

It is clear that a robe of righteousness will adorn Christians in heaven but there is something about the white robes you may not realize. There is no place in all of Scripture where anyone receives a white robe except for the saints killed during the tribulation. What is the import of that? It may well be that the robes of righteousness are white but the Word does not make that statement. They are washed, true. Angels have a white garment, true. Saints are clothed in a robe of righteousness, true; but the phrase "white robes" is used only in reference to the saints who have paid the ultimate price during the tribulation. So is there a special robe given to those who have endured to the end and given up their life? There certainly is a reason that Scripture only references the distribution of white robes solely and exclusively to this rather elite group of Christians. While others may get them, God has not seen fit to mention that any-where else in the Word. Is He granting special honor and recognition to those who actually may have earned special honor and recognition?

So I have to ask the question. Why would PTR apolo-gists argue so strongly for a theory or doctrine that would deprive the saints of the blessing, honor and apparent reward that comes with such exceptional service? Again, would it be eternally more beneficial to go to heaven without having to go through tribulation or is it eternally more beneficial to go to heaven having endured trials and sufferings and to do so successfully without renouncing our Lord even unto death? If there were any correlation at all between earthly service and heavenly rewards, would this not be the circumstance for extra reward? Obviously that is a question for God but so far, these two passages would indicate that He has provided us the answer.

Now consider what Revelation 7:9-17 (KJV), states:

> 9 After this I beheld, and, lo, a great multitude, which no man could number, of all nations, and kindred's, and people, and tongues, stood before

the throne, and before the Lamb, clothed with white robes, and palms in their hands;

10 And cried with a loud voice, saying, Salvation to our God which sitteth upon the throne, and unto the Lamb.

11 And all the angels stood round about the throne, and *about* the elders and the four beasts, and fell before the throne on their faces, and worshipped God,

12 Saying, Amen: Blessing, and glory, and wisdom, and thanksgiving, and honour, and power, and might, *be* unto our God forever and ever. Amen.

13 And one of the elders answered, saying unto me, What are these which are arrayed in white robes? and whence came they?

14 And I said unto him, Sir, thou knowest. And he said to me, These are they which came out of great tribulation, and have washed their robes, and made them white in the blood of the Lamb.

15 Therefore are they before the throne of God, and serve him day and night in his temple: and he that sitteth on the throne shall dwell among them.

16 They shall hunger no more, neither thirst any-more; neither shall the sun light on them, nor any heat.

17 For the Lamb which is in the midst of the throne shall feed them, and shall lead them unto living fountains of waters: and God shall wipe away all tears from their eyes.

Again, we have tribulation saints who have died. While the passage does not directly identify them as having been killed during the tribulation, it would indeed be an extremely unusual passage, if not an oddity of significant proportions, to reference those who died of natural causes during the tribulation to be particularly singled out for special recognition. It is possible that they may well have gone through intense persecution for the cause of Christ but did not happen to die for it. Suffice it to say that no Christian is going to have an easy go of it during the tribulation whether or not their life ends with formal or informal capital punishment. In any event, the Christians' defense of the Gospel and faith in their Savior has earned them white robes and a place of special recognition in Scripture.

So we have tribulation saints receiving white robes prior to the resurrection of the dead and the rapture of the church, all without any reference to any other Christians being so decorated. There is a pattern here. And again, it is troublesome that the PTR apologists work to present an end-time scenario in which the avoidance of persecution and tribulation is somehow preferable to having the privilege of suffering for the Gospel, and that at a level not only providing special recognition but special reward. The next passage for those Christians who are killed during the tribulation comes with even more unique rewards.

Revelation 20: 4-6 (KJV), states as follows:

> "And I saw thrones, and they sat upon them, and judgment was given unto them: and *I saw* the souls of them that were beheaded for the witness of Jesus, and for the word of God, and which had not worshipped the beast, neither his image, neither had received *his* mark upon their foreheads, or in their hands; and they lived and reigned with Christ a thousand years. But the rest of the dead did not live again until the thousand years were finished. This is the first resurrection. Blessed and holy is he who has part in the first resurrection. Over such the second death has no power, but they shall be priests of God and of Christ and shall reign with Him a thousand years."

Here we have yet another example of the honor given to the tribulation saints who die for the cause. They refuse the mark and in staying true to God, their reward is to be beheaded. But their heavenly reward is in the fact that they rule and reign with Christ for a thousand years. You might say, "no big deal" because all the saints rule and reign with Christ for a thousand years. But let's work through this passage.

First, I think it's safe to say that there can only be one *first* resurrection. Clearly the PTR apologists conclude that the only first resurrection we can have is a PTR resurrection as stated in I Thessalonians 4. But, consider the only chronology of events possible without playing a theological version of *Twister*. These saints that are beheaded are clearly killed during the tribulation since the reason for their execution is, in part, their refusal to take the mark of the beast. But their reward is living and reigning with Christ for a thousand years. We know that there can only be one *first* resurrection. And we know that to qualify for ruling and reigning with Christ for a thousand years you have to be part of that first resurrection. So then, how can these tribulation saints rule and reign with Christ and be part of the first resurrection if the first resurrection took place in a PTR before these tribulation saints even had a chance to die? Don't you have to die first in order to be resurrected? At least that's how I have always thought it worked.

Second, Revelation 20:6 states the blessed and holy are those who take part in the first resurrection. The implication is that if you are not part of the first resurrection then you aren't blessed and holy. So according to PTR doctrine, these saints who accept Jesus as Lord during the tribulation and who have obviously missed the PTR are now beheaded and must play second fiddle to those saints who escaped having to die for their faith. In fact some of the PTR saints may have died without ever having been seriously put to the test for their faith. Not only that, but according to Verse 6 these tribulation saints are now subject to the second death since that passage states that blessed are those who take part in the first resurrection upon which the second death has no power. Since the tribulation saints missed the PTR (the first resurrection), apparently they now participate in the second death and second resurrection. Looking at the clear language of Verse 14, those that die a second death are thrown into the lake of fire! This is a perfect example of how the PTR theory simply cannot accommodate the natural flow of the text without severe and torturous convolution.

No PTR apologist would agree to this conclusion of course. The fact is, however, that by their own reasoning and the logical extension of their arguments, the saints killed during the tribulation end up in hell because they missed the first resurrection. They certainly don't mean this but here is where the literal, chronological order of Scripture provides clarity. It is why the PTR interpretation often requires convoluted reasoning and the concurrent reordering of an otherwise straightforward chronology of events to get to its desired destination.

So how does this all square with the obvious interpretation of the text in Revelation 20:4-6 that accords these tribulation saints great honor? Of course, it does not. It's actually somewhat mind-boggling just to unpack the convolution. But the answer to this confusion is simple. Many saints are beheaded for their testimony and steadfastness in resisting the anti-Christ and refusing to take the mark of the beast. At the <u>end</u> of the tribulation, we have our one and only *first* resurrection that includes not only the saints executed during the tribulation but all the saints who have ever died along with all those who are living and remain that are raptured soon thereafter. Thus, all saints take part in this first resurrection directly or indirectly, including those whose rapture is intimately connected with that first resurrection as set forth in I Thessalonians 4. All of these saints rule and reign with Jesus for a thousand years. It is just that simple.

CHAPTER 12

FOR THE JEWS ONLY?

In pointing out that the tribulation is a time of "Jacob's trouble," PTR apologists will frequently attempt to show that a PTR of the saints is the necessary event to clear the way for the Lord to deal with the nation of Israel. Jews generally, and Israel specifically, are unquestionably in Satan's crosshairs during the tribulation. The evil one is after the Jews and he sets up his seat of authority in Jerusalem during the tribulation following the "abomination of desolation." This does not in any way indicate however, that he is *only* after Jews and Israel. That may be his headquarters but his seat of power certainly neither confines his activities nor limits his targets.

Today, we continue to witness the migration of Jews from around the world back to Israel in what is known in Hebrew as *aliyah.* It seems that God has allowed growing persecution against the Jews as part of His plan to bring them home. The departure of Jews out of Europe and especially countries such as France, due to their increasing submission to Islamic culture, has caused a spike in emigration of proportions not seen since WWII. Doubtless, Satan supports the idea since even Islamists talk about how they actually prefer that all Jews return to Israel because that will make their elimination much easier. The satanic malignancy that has defined Iran's leaders for some time is an expression of this attitude whereby they clearly do not deplore a growing Jewish population in Israel due to migration. Rather they applaud it. That way there will be only one sea, the Mediterranean, into which they will need to drive the Jews and not all the oceans around the world.

Unless one considers all the Gentile saints executed during the tribulation to be irrelevant in this analysis, it is clear that the tribulation events are not all about Israel. If the anti-Christ more or less rules the world during the tribulation (as everyone agrees that he does), then in the implementation of what we refer to as his "one world government," his reach of persecution is as pervasive as the earth itself. So who else is the anti-Christ pursuing all over the world? Go look in the mirror. Unless you started this book with this chapter, you have certainly read all the verses dealing with the tribulation, persecution and execution of the saints during the tribulation. Those saints are by no means exclusively Jews. All Israel will be saved as the Apostle Paul points out, but not yet and not until the very end. Those who the anti-Christ pursues through-out the tribulation clearly include lovers of Jesus Christ as well.

For example, consider yet another passage, Revelation 13:7-8(NKJV), wherein it states:

> "It was granted to him (the beast or anti-Christ) to make war with the saints and to overcome them. And authority was given him over every tribe, tongue and nation. All who dwell on the earth will worship him, whose names have not been written in the Book of Life of the Lamb slain from the foundation of the world."

Two considerations should be noted. First, this is not about an attack against the Jews generally or even the 144,000 Jews marked for preservation in Revelation 7. In fact, there is not even a hint of aggression in this passage against Jews or the nation of Israel. Keep in mind that this is no low-level skirmish. It is described as war, a matter of no small undertaking by the enemy. This is an all-out assault with a worldwide scope against those who believe in Jesus Christ-the saints. Second, it appears that the enemy gains a temporary victory or advantage since he "overcomes" them, presumably meaning execution since execution is consistent with the manner by which the anti-Christ deals with the "Christian problem" well-documented in other passages cited in this book.

So it baffles me that very shortly after every Christian in the entire world is supposedly raptured according to the PTR doctrine, the anti-Christ begins a worldwide war against Christians all of whom just got evacuated. War is not waged against those few in number. You use swat teams for that. The fact that the war is worldwide further underscores the extent and number of Satan's enemies. Somehow, all these Christian targets are present during the tribulation even though all Christians just got done being raptured? The PTR answer is that these hundreds of thousands of Christians must represent those who accepted the Lord immediately after the PTR. Nothing in Scripture even hints at this possibility. Of course to bridge this gulf in reason, PTR apologists have to fall back on a supposed, if not imaginary (since it isn't supported anywhere in Scripture) campaign of unbelievably aggressive and successful worldwide evangelism that occurs immediately after the tribulation starts. This is necessary to quickly produce a worldwide population of Christians of sufficient number to wage war against around the entire globe.

If the tribulation just took out all those saints and, at least for a moment, there isn't a single Christian in the whole world, then who carries out this effort? Enter the 144,000 Jews marked for preservation. PTR theory assumes that they are all super anointed Billy Graham's covering the globe to lead this revival. Ignoring the fact that they are likely all in Israel with their attention devoted to their own nation, the

Scripture says absolutely nothing about them regarding any evangelistic activity, let alone worldwide
evangelism. But this is the only way PTR apologists
can explain the phenomenon of all Christians leaving
the earth at the PTR and then, very shortly thereafter,
the world being filled with so many Christians that the
anti-Christ is compelled to wage worldwide war against
them.

One more thing before we move on. Worldwide evangelism is not what is happening during the tribulation in
any event because the Word says it does not happen.
The PTR explanation is not only entirely implausible;
it's not even possible. From Matthew 24, we know that
the last days are marked, not by a passion for the
Gospel but by a coldness within humanity for it says
that the love of many shall grow cold. The trend line
for the Gospel is not up but down during the tribulation. While there are no doubt some people "getting
saved" (those precious few who are attracted to something people are willing to die for), it is generally a time
of cold, not heat for the Lord. Second, it's clear from
II Thessalonians 2 that what is happening during the
tribulation is not worldwide evangelism. It says that
the unveiling of the anti-Christ will be marked by a
great "falling away" which, by definition, is not a great
"coming to."

Though it requires little explanation, worldwide apostasy is the opposite of worldwide evangelism. After all,

would this not be the reason and the time referenced by Jesus in John 9:4 where he stated that He needed to work while it is light because the time will come when no man can work? What other time in the history of the world would fit this admonition than during the tribulation? During the tribulation not only do people fear for their lives but also many are actually abandoning the Gospel. So, where does Satan get this great enemy that needs to be vanquished worldwide? It's called the church that is still here because it never left in a PTR.

The Book of Joel Chapter 2:27-28 (KJV), states that in the last days there will be a great outpouring of the Holy Spirit. In describing those days the passage states as follows:

> "And it shall come to pass afterward that I will pour out my Spirit upon all flesh: and your sons and your daughters shall prophesy, your old men shall dream dreams, your young men shall see visions. And also upon the servants and upon the handmaids in those days will I pour out my Spirit."

Joel 2:23 states that God had given Israel the "former rain moderately and he will cause to come down for you the rain, the former rain, and the latter rain in the first month." Peter, in Acts 2, restates part of this passage and James restates the remainder of this passage in James 5:17. So there will be an even greater outpouring of the Holy Spirit at the *end* of the last days than at the beginning of the last days (upper room). This is because the latter rain consists not only of the initial rain (initial outpouring in the upper room) at the beginning of Pentecost, but a latter outpouring of the Holy Spirit (rain) as well.

The birthing of Christianity in first century Jerusalem originated with little initial persecution. Jesus was the first to be persecuted and that was less because of His message and more because of jealous Jewish leaders regarding his rise in popularity. It is doubtful that the message itself would have been a problem had the message not led to people looking to someone else for spiritual guidance rather than to their religious leaders

There was no *initial* barrier to the germination of the Gospel. Indeed, the 3,000 who accepted Yeshua as Lord, all in one day, are a testament to that fact. The Gospel, however, didn't *spread* without persecution. Its success led to persecution for the simple reason that success is always followed by an opposite and equal reaction coming from those who are threatened by the success of others in which the offended have no role or participation. The offended were initially the Jewish religious leaders. The formal political and civil opposition came later as the population of believers was perceived to be a potentially potent political force.

There was no initial formal opposition awaiting the Gospel's arrival by the civil authorities because there was initially, nothing to fear. That is not the situation in the end times. The persecution is worldwide and there will be no place to flee. No geographic region will be unaware of the power of the Gospel.

Peter, as referenced in the cited passage, was discussing the outpouring of the Holy Spirit that would identify the latter days. Pentecost was the early rain or outpouring. That initial rain was the seed of evangelism sown in the upper room when the Holy Spirit was given. The latter rain is an even greater outpouring and manifestation of the power of the Holy Spirit that comes to complete the harvest and even now is in process. The untold number of millions of people from Asia, the Middle East, Africa and elsewhere who are coming to the saving knowledge of Jesus Christ is the very manifestation of this outpouring of latter rain.

But just as there was ultimately political reaction to the first rain there will be an even greater political reaction to the latter rain because the latter rain is a greater rain. The more the Gospel spreads, the more its influence. The more its influence, the more those not submissive to the Holy Spirit feel threatened. The more the political establishment is threatened, the more persecution that follows. This most certainly includes the anti-Christ himself who comes on the scene at what might be the very pinnacle of church growth.

But when I say church growth, I mean the body of Christ, not physical brick and mortar growth. The effects of signs, wonders and the spread of the Gospel will not go unnoticed by the anti-Christ before his unveiling halfway through the last seven years. The Gospel may well enjoy "success" until the anti-Christ's unveiling and that success is somewhat expected pursuant to the passage from Joel. However, *daylight* ends and then comes the time of darkness "when no man can work."

The jealousy that provoked the religious Jews to persecute Jesus, Paul, Stephen and others may well increase during the first half of the tribulation when the persecution is less intense. But, when the anti-Christ observes the full threat of Christianity, things will take a turn. The falling away or apostasy is a result of the anti-Christ's influence (during the first three and one-half years) and his open persecution (during the last three and one-half years). The saints are persecuted worldwide because the anti-Christ perceives them to be a worldwide menace and a challenge to his authority. But the growth of this "Christian" menace is part of that outpouring beginning before his unveiling. It is not a movement that starts from scratch (as in zero) right after a supposed PTR when there are no believers on the earth because they all have recently vacated lock, stock and barrel.

Finally, we will take a brief look at Revelation Chapter 12. This relatively short chapter provides a concise overview of Satan's hatred of Israel, the Jews and yes, Christians. Satan hates Israel because the land of Israel is the birthplace of Jesus. The Jews were established as God's "chosen people" and Satan pursues the Jews via atrocities such as the Holocaust. But note the very last verse of Revelation 12:17 (NKJV), which, not coincidentally, is chronologically set among the final acts of Satan and states as follows:

> "And the dragon (Satan) was enraged with the woman (Israel), and he went to make war with the rest of her offspring, who keep the commandments of God and have the *testimony of Jesus Christ.*"

Satan hates Israel and everything that originated with Israel. Keeping "the commandments" might include a group broader than Christians (i.e., orthodox Jews) but the offspring of Israel (since it gave birth to Jesus) clearly includes Jesus and then all those who love him ("have the testimony of Jesus Christ"). So yes, the target is Israel but since he hates everything Israel had any role in producing he also hates Christians. Christians are a product of a Jewish Messiah. Because their number far exceeds the number of Jews, Satan may well look at all the Christians as the "monster" produced by Israel. Israel's offspring greatly exceeds, in number, Israel itself.

Then from Chapter 7 of Daniel we read the prophecy of the end times dealing with both the extensive nature of the anti-Christ's reign (Daniel 7:23 says he shall devour the whole earth) as well as the identification of his target. It states in Daniel 7:21-22 (KJV), specifically referring prophetically to the anti-Christ, that he

> "made war against the saints, and prevailed against them; Until the Ancient of Days (our Lord) came, and judgment was given to the saints of the most High: and the time came that the saints possessed the kingdom."

Several things emerge so clearly from this passage. First, there are saints on the earth at the very last days. Second, they are in tribulation since the anti-Christ is out from behind the curtain and is making war against them and winning. Third, Jesus returns to give the saints the victory by coming to rescue them. This is the rapture that clearly happens at the end of the tribulation since the saints have been engaged in a defensive battle with the anti-Christ for some time. Obviously, there can't be a PTR because the saints aren't fighting the anti-Christ at a time before the beginning of the tribulation. This passage makes it clear to the contrary. In the PTR scenario, they are supposedly taken out before all that begins (otherwise what is the point of a PTR). Since the anti-Christ isn't even fully revealed until the middle of the tribulation, he can't kill saints worldwide before the tribulation starts. Fourth, this is a battle against the saints over the whole earth (anti-Christ devours the whole world). It is therefore not a localized battle focused solely upon Jews in and around the Holy Land. The saints are all the saved, not just Jews. They are the targets of the beast along with Israel. The beast appears to have the upper hand but the Captain of the Host comes (descends) and they are saved (raptured) at the time of His second coming.

In summary, the Body of Christ goes into the tribulation without a rapture and provides the ready and necessary target for the anti-Christ along with Israel upon his unveiling one-half way through the tribulation. Many are executed and have the unique opportunity of proving their love for the Lord. Satan is animated not only because of Christians' staunch alliance with the nation of Israel but also because Israel produced Jesus and Jesus produced a whole bunch of saints. The anti-Christ takes out his vengeance against the Christians who have been his worst nightmare for several thousand years and against Israel as well. He can do that only because God has allowed him to by limiting the work of the otherwise restraining influence of the Holy Spirit. When the Holy Spirit stands down for an appointed period of time, the anti-Christ gets to stand up - at least for a little while.

CHAPTER 1

THE ALMOST FORGOTTEN CHAPTER

I recently watched several sermons by a very popular and well-known preacher at a huge (and filled) church. He was preaching on the end times and I almost wept at the degree of scriptural misunderstanding to which this pastor had succumbed. He was both sincere and sincerely wrong. Each time he would tell the thousands in the congregation that they didn't have to worry about that which he was going to teach because they would be plucked out of here before things fell apart, the congregation would cheer.

That experience compelled the inclusion of this chapter. The rapture could happen at any moment he said, because nothing was necessary to first occur. They would be as surprised as anyone since "that day" of the rapture would happen without warning. Key to this proposition and proof of the certainty of a surprise rapture was the passage he cited from Luke 17:26-30 (KJV), which reads as follows:

"And as it was in the days of Noah, so shall it be also in the days of the Son of man. They did eat, they drank, they married wives, they were given in marriage, until the day that Noah entered into the ark, and the flood came, and destroyed them all. Likewise also as it was in the days of Lot; they did eat, they drank, they bought, they sold, they planted, they build; But the same day that Lot went out of Sodom it rained fire and brimstone from heaven, and destroyed *them* all."

The preacher's point was that Jesus himself stated that life would be "normal" at the time of the rapture (eating, drinking and marrying). All things would simply carry on as they had been and hence the surprise of His return. In that context, he encouraged the congregation to not worry about the events around them, instead telling them to go about their lives as they always have. They should marry, buy homes, build and plant, bear children, go to the movies and coffee shops and simply carry on in daily life. According to the preacher's teaching, Jesus was saying that it would just be everyday life until the Lord's return and that they could expect no meaningful changes in their lives or life routines. Nor should there be any particular concern since it was (supposedly) promised that they would exit before any cataclysmic events came their way. And the foregoing passage was the pastor's proof.

On the surface this sounds correct but it is a clear misunderstanding of this entire passage. What Jesus was saying was that to those *who would perish*, life would seem entirely normal. Simple questions will make the point. What was normal, day-to-day life in the world while Noah was building the ark? From Genesis Chapter 6 we know that there was sexual debauchery instigated by fallen angels. We know that the world was filled with violence and so much so that God was sorry that he had created man. God had had it and was preparing to erase humanity. That's how bad it was. Life on earth had to go on with people eating and drinking and building of course, but the world was a terrible place. In other words, terrible had become normal. Otherwise, why would God desire to destroy it? Why would He have been sorry to have created it? Just because life "goes on" doesn't mean it's normal to those who serve the Lord. To the contrary, life without any meaningful disruption in daily routines would only have been normal for a civilization racing to hell. Even as I write, I watch this great country go down a rat hole one day at a time. Yes we still eat, drink, marry, build, etc., because we must, but America's "new normal" is not normal to God nor to God's children. One must finally ask the question that if things were so normal for a righteous Noah, why was the ark even necessary? And why did God, immediately upon Noah entering into the ark proceed to destroy everything? "Normal" could not have been more abnormal to one with a heart for the Lord.

And then there's Lot, the other reference point. How normal were Sodom and Gomorrah at the time of Lot's deliverance? Yes they ate (they had to); they drank (they had to); they got married (I wonder what those relationships were like) but this was the city that wanted to sodomize two angels. These are the two angels who came down to destroy the cities because of a cry that reached all the way to heaven for their wickedness. These are the citizens who after having been blinded by an angel still did not repent. No, they simply kept trying to find the doorknob to Lot's door so that they could continue their homosexual welcome-wagon. Yes, it was normal day-to-day life for Sodom and Gomorrah; let's just sodomize whoever comes into town.

The fact is that it wasn't just a regular life for the one righteous man in town. It says of Lot that his soul was "vexed daily" for all the wickedness of this place. Doesn't sound to me as though he just went to the coffee shop, did his errands and enjoyed life in the quaint and serene towns of Sodom and Gomorrah. Nothing there was normal for Lot, but from the text it appears to have been normal and desirable to his wife and the rest of the town. Yes, life was so normal and regular that God destroyed it with fire and brimstone on the *very day* they left town and Lot's wife gets "salted" on her way out. Just another day like the day God destroyed the earth.

So let's reconsider. The two examples Jesus uses as to what the world would be like immediately before His return are the only two examples in Scripture of wholesale destruction for the then-existing wickedness. That is the real clue. At the time of Jesus' return the rapture will have just previously occurred. There will be a world so horribly sinful that it must be dealt with on a wholesale basis. It will be a world, as in the days of Noah and Lot, so ripe for judgment, that the Christians, as with Lot and Noah, will be extricated immediately before that judgment. It will be due for judgment and Christians will be raptured <u>right</u> before the hammer falls, just as it was in the days of Noah and Lot. Now the Christians, for a change, get to enjoy *a* new normal.

The fact that life isn't even remotely close to what this preacher (and others) proclaim right up to the time of the rapture is yet evident from another passage. II Thessalonians 1:4-7 (KJV), states as follows:

> "...we ourselves glory in you in the churches of God for your patience and faith in all your <u>persecutions</u> and <u>tribulations</u> that ye endure. Which is a manifest token of the righteous judgment of God, that ye may be counted worthy of the kingdom of God, for which ye also <u>suffer</u>: Seeing it is a righteous thing with God to recompense tribulation to them that trouble you; And to you who are troubled, <u>rest</u> with us, when the

Lord Jesus shall be revealed from heaven with his mighty angels."

Notice here that when the Lord returns, it is to give rest to those who have been persecuted and enduring tribulation and suffering. Nothing here suggests that at the time of the rapture (the reward of "rest" as Jesus called it) Christians will be removed *before* they have to endure persecution, tribulation and suffering. Instead the rapture is <u>*because*</u> they have endured persecution, tribulation and suffering. Why would rest be necessary when no activity has occurred warranting rest?

All of this is to underscore the fact that the world of buying, selling, planting, marrying, etc., may appear to give a sense of normalcy regarding the time of Jesus' return. But in fact, normalcy is everyday wickedness to the wicked from which the saints will be given rest, just like Noah and Lot. Normal for the wicked is different than normal for the saints. Yes it will seem normal to the wicked but that's why the day of the Lord takes them as a thief in the night and not the saints. While the Word doesn't reveal what Noah had to deal with regarding his unrighteous neighbors, the Word does tell us that Lot had his challenges. All it took was one event of standing up on behalf of the two angels that visited him (to stop the homosexuals there from attempting to sodomize the angels) and the townsfolk were ready to do to him even worse than what they had in store for the angels.

In summary, Jesus wasn't describing a pleasant, normal, everyday life from this passage in Luke. To the contrary, He was contrasting the reality for the saints (a hostile anti-God world) to a world of apparent normalcy (wrapped in debauchery and wickedness for those that are perishing). That He did so is evident from the fact that He uses two incredibly, judgment-ripe times to set that stage of removal for extricating His saints immediately prior to pouring out the cup of wrath.

CHAPTER 14

THE ALMOST FORGOTTEN VERSE

This will be short and to the point because the verse to follow single-handedly eliminates the PTR theory as a viable explanation of when we, the Christians, exit planet Earth. When I say the verse has been forgotten, I think I'm being charitable. In all likelihood, it's been ignored. The verse is Mark 13:27 (NKJV), which states as follows:

> "And then He (Jesus) will send His angels and gather together His elect from the four winds, from the farthest part of earth to the farthest part of heaven."

Your response may be "So what." To begin, the preceding verses starting with Mark 13:13 reveal that we are obviously dealing with a point in time subsequent to the halfway point of the tribulation since it involves the command to flee when people see the abomination of desolation. This is followed by Mark 13:19, which says, "For in those days there will be tribulation such as has not been since the beginning of creation...nor ever shall be." So this is it, the big one. There can be no dispute that Jesus is talking about the Great Tribulation and a point in time subsequent to the half-way mark in the tribulation, not a point in time 7 years before His return. Subsequent warnings are given by Jesus in subsequent verses and by Mark 13:24 we have reached the point where the sun and moon go dark. Jesus makes it clear that this happens after the tribulation just described as He says, "...after that tribulation the sun will be darkened and the moon will not give its light."

He then states in Mark 13:26 that "Then (when?-after all the things you just read happen), they will see the Son of Man coming in the clouds with great power and glory." Yes it is clearly Jesus second coming and not a halfway trip with a u-turn seven years earlier. Now back to our key verse, Mark 13:27 and here it is again to get the full import. "And then (when?-after all the things you just read including verse 26 happen), He will send His angels, and gather together His elect from the four winds, from the farthest part of earth to the farthest part of heaven."

This completely and perfectly describes the rapture passage from I Thessalonians 4. The trumpet blows and Jesus descends with angels and joins saints from all over heaven along with saints all over the earth who were just raised, including those who were just raptured. After all, we are talking about all the saints here.

From my studies, it appears that PTR apologists deal with this passage in Mark two ways. One way is to contend that the "elect" referenced are all Jews but that was demystified in Chapter 12. But for a moment, accept their claim and then apply it to this passage. If this is only talking about Jews, then at the end of the age, Jesus returns only for the Jews. If this is not a reference to or has application then to non-Jewish believers who die during the tribulation, then either those saints get short shrift or all the saints that die for the Lord in the tribulation must be Jews. This is unsupportable. According to PTR doctrine then the Gentile Christians who die in the tribulation missed the PTR and now they get bumped from this rapture. According to this "Jews=elect" assumption, the angels then are only collecting living and dead Jews from all over heaven and all over earth. So this would then be a second rapture or more appropriately named, the Jewish rapture. It also then implies that all Messianic Jews that died before the first rapture missed the first rapture because the first rapture was only for Gentiles. I must stop here since the implications of this application simply become mind-boggling in what I can only describe as a desperate attempt to explain away the inconvenient truth of this passage in Mark.

The second way this passage is addressed by PTR apologists is to not address it. This is a parallel passage to Matthew 24 but with one slight nuance. Matthew 24:31 makes reference to Jesus' return with the elect from the four winds, from one end of heaven to the other. However, Matthew 24 makes no reference to Jesus collecting saints from all over the <u>earth</u>, only from all over heaven. Matthew 24:31 isn't wrong; it is simply incomplete. It's not unusual for parallel passages in the Gospels to address different aspects of the same event, one emphasizing certain things while another writer emphasizes different aspects of the same event. They complement each other, without contradicting each other.

It would be as if a husband said that his wife wore a blue dress the night before at church and another party said that the husband's wife was wearing a pretty scarf with shoes to match. There is no contradiction. It simply depends upon what part of the story being related that the speaker desires to emphasize. But, here, both Gospels need to be considered to get the full picture.

So, if you didn't want to reference the fact that Jesus, at His second coming, not only collects saints from all over heaven, <u>but also collects them from all over the earth</u>, you would only quote the Matthew 24:31 passage. The quote from Matthew would then nicely fit the PTR paradigm. The reason the passage in Matthew allows for a PTR is precisely because no earth-bound saints are referenced. And why wouldn't they be referenced? To the PTR apologist, it's obvious, they leave in the PTR. They won't be around on earth at the end of the tribulation just as the Son of Man readies Himself to return. Matthew 24:31 then becomes a proof text of a PTR but the inconvenient existence of Mark 13:27, with more clarity and explanation eclipses and frankly, shatters the PTR assumptions drawn from using only the passage in Matthew to address this topic. The saints on earth are clearly drawn up at approximately the same time as the dead are raised and specifically at Jesus' second coming. Only an arbitrary and brutal reordering of events from this Scripture could have this take place before the tribulation. Because the saints on earth are included in the passage from Mark as part and parcel of Jesus' return constitutes what is called in law, "summary judgment." It means no further discussion is necessary nor additional evidence required for the truth of the matter is obvious. The saints collected from earth along with the saints collected from heaven (more or less simultaneously) can only be interpreted in the context of a post-tribulation rapture.

Just follow the chronology of events in this chapter and it's so very clear. We go through tribulation. Some of us survive and some of us don't. But we all join Jesus just before His return at the end of the tribulation. Pretty simple.

To ignore the clear chronology of events from this passage is inexcusable. Why is the passage that completely and with great specificity in describing exactly what happens when Jesus returns at the end of the tribulation not the passage of choice when explaining these end-time events?

CHAPTER 15

THE LAST STANDING ARGUMENT-NOAH

The story of Noah is much written about in PTR articles as a supposed bulletproof argument support-ing the PTR. It goes like this. Noah escapes the death of civilization having been removed from harm's way. Ergo, it's a prototype of a rapture, specifically a PTR. The story is only proof of a PTR if one ignores evidence to the contrary.

The first point is the least of three points I will make but it's a point that I have never heard discussed and is worth noting. Eight people were saved on the Ark; Noah, his wife, three sons and their wives. However, the spiritual state of everyone other than Noah is never mentioned. Only Noah is mentioned as being righteous (several times). Whether everyone else was or wasn't righteous becomes more relevant the more the PTR advocates contend this event to be a prototype of a PTR. Why? Quite obviously, the unsaved are not whisked away by flood or in any rapture, pre or post-trib. So if some of Noah's family were not righteous, how can this be the supposed prototype that the PTR advocates contend? If this story is not intended to reflect a rapture at all (pre or post-trib), then the spiritual state of Noah's family is a non-issue.

So did Noah's family enjoy a coattail grace for the sole purpose of post-flood procreation or were they all righteous too? It would seem that Scripture would have referenced their righteousness also if Noah were not the only righteous one. If you must be righteous to make the rapture and the ark represents the rapture, then PTR advocates are forced to conclude that everyone on the boat was righteous; however, there is no scriptural basis for such a conclusion. Furthermore, the ark as a rapture prototype becomes yet more problematic when we discover that one of Noah's sons, Ham, (who made the ark "rapture") implicitly engaged in, at the least, some form of sexual attraction upon seeing his father naked. Whatever it was, it was enough to trigger a prophetic curse through Ham to Ham's son, Canaan and on down the line.

True, this all occurred after Ham "got off the boat." But the rapture ruptures if you have unrighteous people "making the boat." All this may be a matter of "disputing doubtful things" as Scripture says, but it has relevance if the PTR theory necessitates believing in a doubtful thing.

Second, Noah and his family did not *escape* as in being removed. They weren't caught up or delivered *from* the earth but rather were preserved *in the midst* of the situation. This is a point made earlier in several other contexts but needs to be raised again. As such, if anything, the story of Noah more precisely describes not being removed but, instead, actually being present and protected.

Third and critical to the discussion, the tribulation is what Satan throws at humanity. God's judgment is a different matter. We have been over this before but there is that fundamental distinction between Satan's tribulation (i.e. what the anti-Christ does) and God's wrath (i.e. judgment on mankind). So, who brought the flood? Was it God or Satan? PTR advocates have to pick a horse here and ride it. The Noah story can never be a prototype of a PTR removing Christians from Satan's persecution because it wasn't Satan's persecution from which Noah was delivered. It was God's judgment. So if the PTR advocates want to hang on to this alleged irrefutable proof text of a PTR they now have to shift the entire rapture story. From now on, it can no longer be a rapture saving Christians from the anti-Christ and the tribulation. It must be a rapture saving Christians from God and His judgment. They can't have it both ways. In fact, if the ark "rapture" is interpreted as protection against God's judgment, the obvious implication is that for Satan's persecution (tribulation), Christians are still here since Satan's persecution begins long before God's judgments. My, what a tangled web that's been woven.

CHAPTER 16

WHY IS THE DISCUSSION SO IMPORTANT?

As I mentioned at the beginning, this is a book that I really did not want to write. While the topic is of great personal interest, I never really felt a compelling need to inform people regarding the great preponderance of evidence supporting a post-tribulation rapture; that is, until recently.

But the issue is far more important than I could have imagined for the reasons that will shortly be pointed out. Frankly, there are not a lot of writings regarding a post-tribulation rapture. It is in no small part due to the fact that for hundreds of years across the globe (and especially where there has been intense persecution of Christians), the post tribulation view has been dominant and the assumed interpretation of eschatological events.

But certain events have been a catalyst in the growing burden to get this message out. It was previously mentioned that the great number of PTR advocates believe in a PTR because that is simply what they have been taught. They are innocent, sincere Christians who love God with all their heart. But I have noticed that many tend to parrot that which PTR teachers have taught them regarding end-time events. In fact, many avoid personal study of the Book of Revelation (outside of an "approved" PTR teaching guide), instead, leaving it to the "experts" to explain this complicated book that requires all sorts of charts and graphs to even begin to comprehend. I don't blame them. I love them and their numbers include many friends and even some family members within that group. Frankly, they should be able to rely upon their teachers to some extent, so I understand their perspective.

Then there are the teachers and the pastors, who themselves frequently fall into the same category as their parishioners. They too have sincerely believed but have been taught the PTR doctrine in their theology schools. While there may be some who will only teach a "feel-good" message to keep people coming back, I really do not think very many PTR pastors employ that artifice in this context. I will give them the benefit of the doubt. But they too naturally would want to teach what they would want to hear.

Finally, there is the last group that requires a stern rebuke. They are incessant, if not militant in the advocacy of the PTR. It dominates their writings, their radio programs and their ministries. I have had a radio program for over 10 years and a while ago I placed a call to a ministry-operated station regarding placing my program on the air. The first question from the manager was not even if I was a Christian. No, he wanted to know if I believed in the PTR. When I told him no, I received the left foot of fellowship as though I were a heretic. It is this group to whom I owe this book. Had there not been such excessive advocacy of a PTR, this book would likely not have come to fruition. I so resisted "having" to write this that I have required constant provocation to sustain the effort and this radio station contributed to the project.

It is not worth debating when the first PTR literature arose. PTR apologists attempt to point to some early writings, I think in an effort to legitimize their position. But there is no question that the *popularity* of the PTR perspective was kick-started in the early nineteenth century. The Scofield Bible greatly accelerated its acceptance especially when that bible became the bible of choice used in many theological schools. But ultimately, whether its origins are ancient or it's a Johnny-come-lately theory is actually irrelevant.

A point that does need to be emphasized is the fact that the PTR theory has never been received well nor has it been dominant in any area of the world histori-cally characterized by oppression and persecution of Christians. That is significant. Those who attempt to live out their faith in areas hostile to Christianity and are under present persecution are the ones who, if the PTR were true, would likely believe that they had missed it. It seems that those who have had some exposure to real persecution better understand the fact that when we give our lives to Jesus Christ we have also just enlisted in the Army. It's extended combat. Talk to a Messianic Jew who has orthodox parents or Muslims who become born again out of strong Islamic families. They know that they entered that combat zone when they announced their Christian identity and that they may not get out alive.

But the converse is true also. Those who live in areas that have had little or no persecution are where the PTR position is the most readily and eagerly embraced. Not having had to deal with the tough side of the walk with Jesus, there is a readiness to find an exit strategy that maintains their status quo. Enter escapism theology. It's what we want and because it's what we want, it is also what we want to hear. I get it.

All of this explains why the PTR doctrine has had its greatest welcome, growth and expansion inside the United States. Christians here have never really experienced persecution for the sake of the Gospel. They have to go to another country to have that experience. And while it is my sincere hope that this book will change at least some hearts and minds, I have no great illusion in that respect. The fact is that what will most quickly and decidedly change PTR minds in the United States will be a big dose of what's happening elsewhere; hair-raising episodes of their faith being challenged to the point of being sued, persecuted, imprisoned and executed. Actually, other than the outpouring of the Holy Spirit in the upper room, nothing has historically had a greater purifying effect upon the church than persecution. Of course that's not what we want, but I didn't make the rules.

So let's see what God has said that makes this understanding of end-time events so much more critical than one might think. To start let's go to I Peter 4:12 (KJV):

> "Beloved, think it not strange concerning the fiery trial that is to try you as though some strange thing happened to you: But rejoice, inasmuch as ye are partakers of Christ's sufferings; that when his glory shall be revealed, ye may be glad also with exceeding joy."

Notice that the Holy Spirit is telling us through Peter that persecution is the norm, not the exception (even though we have not had that experience here in the U.S.). And it's a fiery trial at that. This is what the Christian world has experienced for ages. So, "pre-tribbers" in the U.S., you should not think it strange to go through a fiery trial on earth. What the Holy Spirit is saying is that we should think it strange to not go through fiery trials. Tribulation is clearly the exception, not the rule. Of course, the PTR perspective is exactly contrary to this passage.

Persecution and tribulation are the norm among most Christians. Actually, they are the two key ways by which we identify with the Lord Jesus Christ. He suffered and since the servant is not greater than the master, then we can expect to suffer also. Did Jesus go through tribulation? Being beaten, spit upon, tortured and crucified would seem to qualify. What we cannot expect is to <u>not</u> go through it. There are some who may get a "hall pass" and skip this experience by God's grace but we cannot expect that someone else's exception should be our norm. We have no basis upon which to expect deliverance as the assumed experience because Scripture does not support that.

Last, but absolutely not least, this passage indicates that these sufferings with Jesus are what qualifies us for experiencing "exceeding joy" when His glory is revealed. Imagine that somehow the degree of joy we experience, upon His revelation, is directly related to how much suffering we have gone through in identifying with His sufferings.

Why this teaching is so important is partly because if we think that suffering is not of God and that His love is primarily reflected in deliverance from tribulation, then that mindset will always have us looking for deliverance in all situations. If we believe that it is not

God's will that we go through tribulation in the last days, would we not also conclude that it is not His will to suffer persecution at any other point along the way? Would we not likely conclude that suffering at any time could just not possibly be in His game plan for us?

Escapism theology will produce an escapism mindset. It is also an inducement to inaction. It will be thought normal to cut and run because after all we haven't been appointed to endure this. So this first point filters down to this. A PTR perspective predisposes us to think in terms of escaping from, not engaging, the enemy. That is so contrary to our calling. It is spiritually debilitating, if not emasculating. Having done all to stand, we turn to escape? The consequence of this is not a strong church but a weak church because as persecution arises, the growing thought will be, "why fight this fight since we will soon be long gone?" Just hold on a little longer and we'll be out of here. So much for occupying until He comes.

Also the PTR theory does not have the impact on evangelism that is often assumed. While there are some great churches that do a good job of soul-winning and who embrace the PTR, the reason for their evangelistic success is not attributed to the teaching of a PTR theory. Soul winning cannot spring from a false premise. It may *appear* that teaching individuals to accept Jesus as Lord is the necessary ingredient to avoid end-time tribulation. The claim is that what is coming is so bad that PTR advocates' efforts will lead people to

Jesus so as to avoid the consequences of inaction. In other words, "get saved" to avoid persecution.

But I must ask a very simple question. If people were not moved to accept Jesus and avoid eternity in the lake of fire then why would they be moved to avoid a few years of tribulation? What is worse, to go through a few years of tribulation on earth (as bad as that may be) or eternity in the lake of fire? Did not the Holy Spirit speaking through Paul state that the tribulation of this world is light compared to the glory that awaits us? If you are not motivated to evangelize with the purpose of helping loved ones avoid hell itself, then is it not a disingenuous motivation for evangelization to just avoid Satan's wrath for a couple of years on earth? Maybe these "converts" really do not believe in a hell. And what happens to this shallow foxhole conversion when the only reason for accepting the Lord proves incorrect? Besides, the convoluted PTR theory is a much more complex scenario of events for the lost person to ever understand than the relatively simple concept of why you want to avoid hell. This is especially so since it requires little teaching to show that hell is a certainty for those who don't receive Jesus Christ as Savior.

Now, let us move to the last and most important point of this chapter. The greatest risk associated with the PTR doctrine is the potential for severe spiritual damage when those who strongly embrace the PTR discover the error. When it will be most apparent to believers that they are in the tribulation is when the "abomination of desolation" occurs in Jerusalem at the three and one-half year mark (halfway) through the tribulation. With no PTR, the beginning of the tribulation period may not be obvious, particularly if things are already in a fast moral decay around the world (in other words, sort of where we are now). Whatever this despicable act of the anti-Christ looks like at the time of this "desecration," believers will now know that they are actually in it - the Great Tribulation.

Upon the realization that they have not been raptured at the time they so believed, and that certain persecution and maybe even death lies before them, then what happens? Do they call up their pastor and ask him what went wrong? Does the pastor in turn call up his professor from Bible school and ask where did he make a left turn? However it plays out there will be a shaking and rattling of peoples' faith. If they only go so far as to blame it on the pastor, it may turn out okay but what happens if they should blame it on God or on His word? What else is in this old Bible that isn't true? If something that is so stressed, impressed and drilled into so many peoples' minds as the assured deliverance of a PTR is in fact, not so assured (as in totally false), then what? The collateral damage to the faithful may not be just collateral; it may be critical. Do they toss their faith when this whole thing goes sideways? Is it, "Yea, hath God really said?" As noted, if the blame is placed on pastors, the situation may be recoverable, but if people blame the Word of God, that is an entirely different situation.

You see, we could spiritually survive a conclusion that God is correct and the Bible is reliable but that some pastors and teachers got it wrong. However, you couldn't spiritually survive a conclusion that those pastors and teachers have correctly interpreted the Bible but the Bible isn't true. In the first scenario, it's man that's at fault. In the second scenario, God is believed to be at fault.

Obviously a post-tribulation rapture believer does not share that risk. If the premise of this book were wrong, I would be thrilled. But the PTR perspective, on the other hand, has the makings of a spiritual nightmare. For those whose fundamental belief in the inerrancy of Scripture is throttled by the revelation that they are still here when they thought they would be removed, the potential fallout is disastrous.

In II Thessalonians 2 the Word states that at the time of the revealing of the anti-Christ there will be a great falling away. We described it before as apostasy, a decided turning away from the Gospel by those who previously embraced it (at least to some degree). Could it be that the faith of those who believe in a PTR is shattered? Do those individuals comprise at least some of those who form this great "falling away?" In fact, is this the cause of their very falling away-that they now see a critical pillar of their theology crumble and they throw in the towel and take the mark of the beast?

Consider for a moment the likely context of Jesus' comment in Matthew 16:25 that "whoever desires to save his life shall lose it, but whoever loses his life for my sake shall find it." We have gone to great lengths to spiritualize this verse, never taking it literally. Why not? Because we have never faced any measure of tribulation in this country that would give this verse its literal meaning. Therefore, we find ways to spiritualize it to try and give it a more "general" application. But remember the life given up by Rachel Joy Scott in the Columbine, Colorado school shooting many years ago. Rachel, having been shot several times was not dead. One of the killers seeing that she yet lived asked her if she still believed in God. Her answer was, "You know I do." And with that he finished her off. She could have said "No I don't any longer, let me live!" and she may have well saved her physical life only to lose her spiritual life by denying Jesus Christ.

Now take such a situation and expand it in time, scope, and geography such that other Christians are facing tribulation leading up to a choice to accept or deny Jesus at gunpoint (whether it's century-to-century persecution that's gone on forever elsewhere) or to take the mark of the beast lest one be killed in the Great Tribulation. What happens to the faith of those who have completely trusted in a PTR (in either situation) to avoid such a situation when that very situation of spiritual and physical death or life arises in the same moment? It will be enough of a challenge for those who are biblically prepared for that moment because of proper instruction but the concern, of course, lies with those whose likelihood of surviving this challenge spiritually is handicapped by bad theology. The risk of denial of our Lord is there and it is a high risk. Further, the more central the PTR belief is to one's faith, the greater the risk of denial becomes.

CHAPTER 17

REMEMBER WHAT'S AT STAKE

Did not the Holy Spirit, speaking through Paul, in Romans 8:18, say that the "sufferings of this present time are not worthy to be compared with the glory which shall be revealed in us?" It seems far too seldom these days that we are reminded of the fact that there really is a heaven and a hell. Before anyone concludes that enduring a tribulation may be too much for them, it would be inspiring and comforting to refresh ourselves on what we are fighting for and why the battle is worth whatever is required.

Revelation 21:4 says that God "shall wipe away all tears from their eyes; and there shall be no more death, neither sorrow, nor crying; neither shall there be any more pain: for the former things have passed away." Think about that for a moment. No death. Wouldn't it be nice to never have to go to another funeral, including your own? Wouldn't it be nice to never have to say "good-bye?" Wouldn't it be nice to be able to leave home and not wonder if you'll ever see your spouse or children again?

People say that God prepares us for death. I suppose that He does and maybe He must. However, the longer I live, the more it seems that He does that by preparing us for a new life. He fuels the growing desire and longing to move on which is not death, but rather fullness of life. We want more life but we do not want more of *this* life. Just consider, no more sorrow and no more crying. No more bad news. No more heartaches, bankruptcies, children in jail, people in hospitals or divorces. No more cancer, psoriasis, fibromyalgia, stroke, heart disease, blindness, deafness, back pain, diabetes, migraines or rotator cuff problems. No more abortion, child molestation, drugs, pornography, robberies, murders or lawsuits. Just think of all the things that cause sorrow, anguish, pain and anger and then just eliminate them. And what are the former things that have passed away? Fear, doubt, worry, anxiety, envy, jealousy, pride, arrogance, lust, hatred, covetousness, well, I think you get the idea. So what is at stake? Absolutely everything.

CHAPTER 18

ARE WE IN THE VERY LAST OF THE LAST DAYS ?

I don't know. I think so.

CHAPTER 19

SO HOW DO WE ENDURE IN THE TRIBULATION?

Jesus said in Matthew 24:13 that those who endure to the end shall be saved. He clearly was not talking about "physical salvation" since enduring to the end implies until one is called home. Logically, you are not saved physically when you die; quite the opposite. So we are talking a spiritual salvation that can only, from the context, be read to mean that if we don't turn our back on Him or deny Him, we will be saved. Some might even say, maintain our salvation.

Suppose that in the course of enduring tribulation, the demand is put forth to a person requiring that he or she recant their faith in Jesus Christ as Lord and Savior if he or she wants to live. All the questions regarding whether one can throw away their salvation or whether they were ever really saved, at that point, become meaningless. If they deny Jesus Christ as Lord, they are done. Jesus minced no words in Matthew 10:32-33 (KJV), where He stated:

"Whosoever therefore shall confess me before men, him I will confess before my Father which is in heaven. But whosoever shall deny me before men, him will I also deny before my Father which is in heaven."

Even Judas, upon realizing the error of his ways could not come back over the threshold he had crossed.

Since the Word is clear that there is no other name under heaven whereby man can be saved than the name of Jesus, if you do not have Jesus, you do not have the Father. If you do not have the Father, you do not have the Father's home. Hell waits. If you worship the beast at all, it's over. If you take the mark of the beast, it's over. If you deny Jesus Christ in the context of swearing allegiance and worship to the beast, it's over. People can argue all day long about what spiritual state precipitates or precedes a denial but it really does not matter. If you deny Jesus at that point and it is part and parcel of changing allegiance to the beast to save your life, then you have just lost your life.

All of this raises anew that pesky question from II Thessalonians 2 about the great falling away and just what is the state of those who commit apostasy and, to save their life, align themselves with the beast. At the least, it brings to mind the passage from Matthew 16:25 (KJV), where Jesus states:

"For whosoever will save his life shall lose it: and whosoever will lose his life for my sake shall find it."

Those who, during the tribulation (or any other time for that matter) deny the Lord in an attempt to save their physical lives will lose their spiritual life. One should not count on the "Peter denial" defense either. Jesus had not died and risen yet at the time of Peter's denial. Since the Holy Spirit had not yet been poured out at Pentecost and into believers he did not yet have the Holy Spirit at that time to restrain or direct his actions. But for Christians today who have the Holy Spirit in them, it's a different story. Those who, before the minions of the anti-Christ, confess Jesus Christ as Lord will suffer irreparable harm on the spot (i.e., death). But in losing their physical life, they will be assured of having gained eternal spiritual life.

It literally comes down to the difference between life and death. Heaven or hell and fortunately, the choices will be extremely clear. So it is a very logical question to ask how one prepares for that time or if preparation is even necessary. Just how do you endure the tribulation?

The first and foremost thing to keep in mind is the admonition set forth in I Corinthians 10 (KJV), where it states in verse 13:

"There hath no temptation (testing) taken you but such as is common to man: but God is faithful, who will not suffer you to be tempted (tested) above that ye are able; but will with the temptation also make a way to escape, that ye may be able to bear it."

As was mentioned before, the escape is not an exit since the Lord provides a way to bear it, endure it or prevail in the midst of it.

This testing and trial will be divided into two broad groups. First, are those challenges and trials that do not involve (or do not *yet* involve) significant physical pain, torture or death. This would include being sued or harassed, confiscation of goods and assets, attempted brainwashing, imprisonment following a trial in a kangaroo court as well as any other form of tribulation falling short of the infliction of meaningful physical pain. For this, no preparation other than time in the Lord is necessary, for Jesus said in Matthew 10:18-19 (KJV):

"And ye shall be brought before governors and kings for my sake, for a testimony against them and the Gentiles. But when they deliver you up, take no thought how or what ye shall speak: for it shall be given you in that same hour what ye shall speak."

The individuals referenced in this passage had already been scourged or beaten so we will address that separately. But as to the inquisitorial aspect of this event the Holy Spirit has been given to us to speak through us. We need no other defense, no articulation of any points, arguments or anything man-made. It will be all God-made.

When the situation involves physical pain or painful death in some manner, then reference needs to again be made to I Corinthians in that God knows what we can handle. Even aside from a tribulation environment, we will experience varying degrees of physical pain that are simply endured. No one gets through this life without experiencing some degree of physical pain. However, we are talking about pain at a level that is not common to man under the most trying of experiences.

Enter the grace of God. Most teachings about grace (by which I mean about 99%) are about the *saving* grace of God. But without diminishing this primary role of God's grace, grace also operates in an area of life that many of us have not experienced. Few of us have had the need to call upon God for this application. It is the grace Paul needed when burdened with the thorn in the flesh from which he sought deliverance three times but was seemingly denied or at least, delayed since the matter was going to be resolved in a way other than what he sought. As described in II Corinthians 12:9 (KJV), the Lord said unto Paul:

> "My grace is sufficient for thee: for my strength
> is made perfect in weakness."

There is no sense in this passage that the Lord is saying to just grin and bear it. God would provide the answer and accomplish victory. By complete submission to God, God would reveal His power to and through Paul in the most trying of circumstances. As a result, Paul would emerge stronger than the way by which Paul originally sought deliverance. At the time of complete submission to the situation is also when control has been surrendered entirely to God. Now God can move in a way that given the weakness of man, His grace has its most profound impact.

Space does not permit to tell of the testimonies of Christians under immense persecution to whom the Lord has provided at their very moment of torture, peace, a calm, a resolve and in some cases, what can only be described as a supernatural deadening of all nerve endings that would otherwise cause one to writhe in pain. One such example comes from one of the greatest books I have ever read, *The Light and the Glory* by Peter Marshall and David Manuel. With this story, no other examples will be necessary.

They tell the story of two Jesuit priests, Jean De Brebauf and his companion Gabriel Lalemant, who were missionaries in the upper Midwest in the 17th century. They had ministered for years to the Huron

Indians but were taken prisoner by the Iroquois, a tribe known for deriving great pleasure from observing their victims struggle in the midst of sadistic rituals of torture. The account picks up after De Brebauf and his companions are tied at the stake:

"The first Iroquois torture was to pour boiling water over Father Brebeuf's naked body, in mockery of the Sacrament of Baptism. When by the grace of God, he denied them the pleasure of hearing him cry out in agony-for the pain of their victims was intoxicating to them-they tied a collar of metal hatchets, heated red-hot, around his neck. Again, Father Brebeuf disappointed them, and so they fastened a belt of birch bark, filled with pitch and resin, around his waist and set it afire. And still he remained dumb before his tormentors, his face set like flint.

Now Father Brebeuf did speak, but not in anguish. He called out encouragement to his fellow captives. Enraged, the Indians cut off his lips and tongue and rammed a hot iron down his throat. Then they cut strips of flesh from his arms and legs and devoured them before his eyes. But as he was dying, Father Brebeuf was gaining the victory, just as had his Savior on the Cross before him, and the Indians sensed it. In the end, they cut his heart out and ate it and drank of his blood, in the hope that they could gain the spirit power that had given him more courage than any man they had ever seen." (Pages 76-77).

Why wasn't De Brebeuf screaming and hollering at the top of his lungs throughout this ordeal? He had not passed out and so, was conscious for the greater part of the torture. Why wasn't he writhing in pain? How was he able to speak in such a controlled manner when parts of his body are on fire?

Similar questions could be asked about Stephen, the very first Christian martyr, who was stoned to death by the religious leaders for his testimony of Jesus Christ. Even as he is being pelted to death, Stephen, with no evidence of anguish or severe pain simply says "Lord Jesus, receive my spirit. Lay not this sin to their charge." As he is dying, there is no screaming, yelling or writhing in pain, but rather a simple plea to forgive his enemies amidst his own personal tribulation.

No biblical story however, paints a more complete picture of the tribulation, fiery trial and post tribulation rapture than the chilling yet exciting similarities of Daniel 3 with Shadrach, Meshach and Abednego in the furnace and the description of the anti-Christ's despotic rule in Revelation 13. Consider the following:

1. Nebuchadnezzar ruled the known world. The anti-Christ will rule the world in the tribulation.
2. Nebuchadnezzar desired to be worshiped. The anti-Christ will desire to be worshiped.
3. Nebuchadnezzar builds an image to be worshiped. The anti-Christ will build an image to be worshiped.
4. Nebuchadnezzar demanded all people to worship the image. The anti-Christ will demand that all people worship the image.
5. The penalty for not worshiping Nebuchadnezzar's image was death. The penalty for not worshiping the image of the anti-Christ will be death.
6. Shadrach, Meshach and Abednego are thrown into a fiery furnace for refusing to worship Nebuchadnezzar's image. Those who refuse to worship the anti-Christ will be subjected to whatever method of torture and execution suits the fancy of the anti-Christ.
7. Shadrach, Meshach and Abednego are delivered not prior to going into the furnace but while in a fiery trial, in fact, a furnace heated seven times its normal heat. God will deliver those in the midst of a fiery trial during the tribulation. It may be with the *form* of grace given to Stephen or in the manner provided to De Brebeuf, or in some other manner.

Of course Shadrach, Meshach and Abednego did not pass away and depart for heaven but emerged from the trial completely unscathed (not even the smell of smoke was upon their bodies). While Christians undergoing persecution may pass away, the similarity to point 7 is striking in the most pertinent way. Shadrach, Meshach and Abednego appeared to have been tortured simply by their presence in the furnace but in fact they never felt any pain. The fire had no impact on their bodies for in some miraculous manner, no sensory nerves in their bodies detected anything abnormal. Likewise, Christians subjected to such persecution in the tribulation will, in their weakness; appear remarkably strong, just like De Brebeuf, just like Stephen and just like Shadrach, Meshach and Abednego.

Can you imagine having said to De Brebeuf, Stephen, or Shadrach, Meshach and Abednego to be encouraged because they will not have to go through the Great Tribulation? So how did they endure? The same way we will endure if that is our lot in life. This is the grace referenced in the passage about Paul and his thorn in the flesh. What Jesus endured on the cross, we do not. If His suffering on the cross is a payment for sin, then one of the collateral benefits of that payment is that the grace He did not enjoy on His cross, is the grace that will be showered upon us when we are upon our own personal "cross." The great substitution that occurred on Calvary will gloriously provide great provision at our time of great need.

The very fact that on the cross Jesus cried out "My God, My God, why hast Thou forsaken Me" should be a clue. He was made to be sin for us so that we might become the righteousness of God. This presents a truth seldom taught in most churches. He became sin on the cross and there was no grace for the sin He became. But we, who are partners in this great exchange, receive the very benefits He forfeited. One of those benefits is miraculously, a God-given grace to withstand what De Brebeuf, Stephen and Shadrach, Meshach and Abednego withstood. He is a miracle-working God after all and we may never feel more alive than in the process of enduring that which under normal circumstances would otherwise be utterly intolerable.

It used to bother me that in reading about Jesus having cried out on the cross as the Son of God to then hear of His children holding up well in some incredibly terrifying circumstances in ways that He didn't appear to on the cross. I dared not even think such thoughts but I was perplexed why He would not be able to bear the pain as well as His children did. The very thought seemed blasphemous until it was revealed to me that He died as one suffering the ravages of dying without the Father. No grace, no communion and no peace, just the pain of separation, nails and humiliation.

Yes, He was sinless but to what advantage on the cross is not knowable to those who do not know Him.

Because He got nothing, we got everything. Now I got it. He got what we deserved and we get what He deserved. Where sin once abounded (as in us), grace now abounded even more and just one of the places that the abounding grace will manifest is when our turn comes to prove just how much we love Him. Remember, there is only one thing you really want to hear at the end of your life. "Well done thou good and faithful servant."

And if you think that it is unfair for Jesus to suffer in a way by which we will not, you are absolutely right. He has provided a way for us to supernaturally avoid or greatly minimize the physical pain He endured on the cross when we are on our "cross." As we noted in I Corinthians 10, Jesus has provided a way to endure when it will be beyond human endurance. Jesus already paid that price so that we might "enjoy" the grace on our cross that He couldn't appropriate on His. There is nothing at all fair about this exchange. That's why it's called "love."

ABOUT THE AUTHOR

Rob Walter is an attorney and graduate of the University of Michigan, Regent Univ. School of Law in Virginia and the University of San Diego School of Law (Master of Law in Taxation). In addition to practicing law in Santa Barbara, CA, Rob also pastors *Valley Harvest Church* and hosts *Red Sky Radio*, a radio program syndicated throughout the southwest where he dissects relevant current topics for listeners challenged by a world that is increasingly hostile to Christianity. Rob's passionate desire is to help listeners be able to think, walk, talk, vote and invest from a biblical perspective. You can hear the program at RedSkyRadio.net and contact him at :

info@RedSkyRadio.net.